MARIA LLOVET

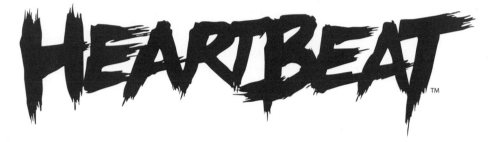
HEARTBEAT™

Published by
BOOM!
STUDIO

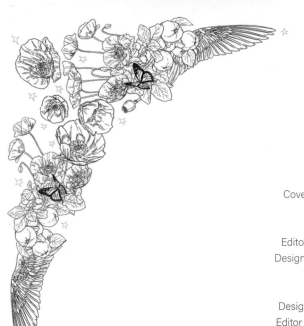

Cover by **MARIA LLOVET**

Spanish Edition
Editor **ANNABEL ESPADA**
Designer **ELENA GONZÁLEZ**

English Edition
Designer **SCOTT NEWMAN**
Editor **AMANDA LaFRANCO**
Executive Editor **SIERRA HAHN**

If you or someone you know is having thoughts of suicide, you can call the National Suicide Prevention Lifeline at **(800) 273-8255**. A caller is connected to a certified crisis center near where the call is placed. The call is free and confidential.

HEARTBEAT, September 2020. Published by BOOM! Studios, a division of Boom Entertainment, Inc. Heartbeat is ™ & © 2015, 2020 Maria Llovet / Represented by Norma Editorial, S.A. Originally published in single magazine form as HEARTBEAT No. 1-5. ™ & © 2019, 2020 Maria Llovet / Represented by Norma Editorial, S.A. All rights reserved. BOOM! Studios™ and the BOOM! Studios logo are trademarks of Boom Entertainment, Inc., registered in various countries and categories. All characters, events, and institutions depicted herein are fictional. Any similarity between any of the names, characters, persons, events, and/or institutions in this publication to actual names, characters, and persons, whether living or dead, events, and/or institutions is unintended and purely coincidental. BOOM! Studios does not read or accept unsolicited submissions of ideas, stories, or artwork.

BOOM! Studios, 5670 Wilshire Boulevard, Suite 400, Los Angeles, CA 90036-5679.
Printed in China. First Printing.

ISBN: 978-1-68415-608-5, eISBN: 978-1-64668-020-7

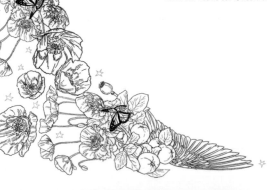

HEART BEAT™

ET·LVX·
IN·TENEBRIS
·LVCET

Story and Art by
MARIA LLOVET

Lettered by
ANDWORLD DESIGN

Translated by
ANDREA ROSENBERG

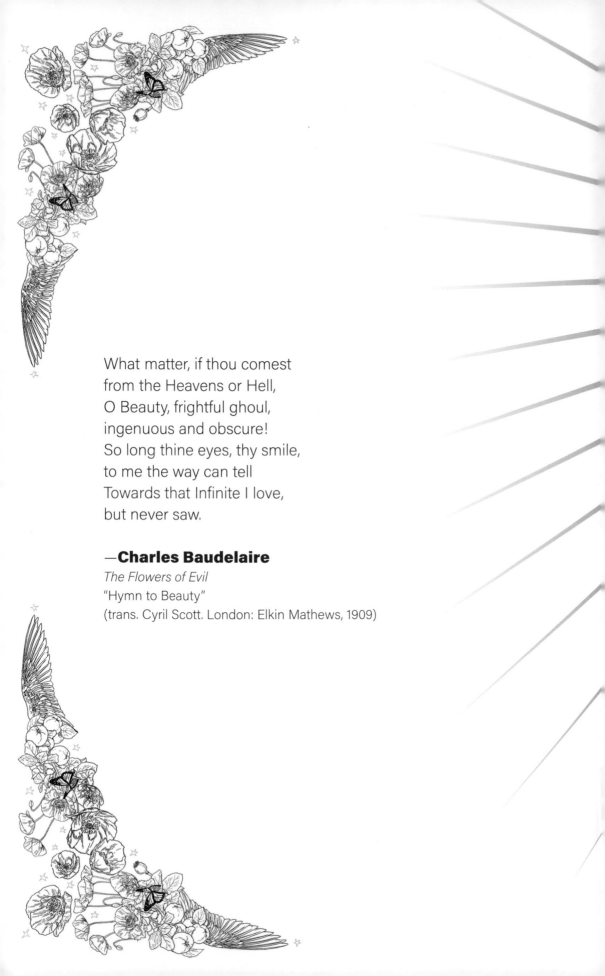

What matter, if thou comest
from the Heavens or Hell,
O Beauty, frightful ghoul,
ingenuous and obscure!
So long thine eyes, thy smile,
to me the way can tell
Towards that Infinite I love,
but never saw.

—Charles Baudelaire
The Flowers of Evil
"Hymn to Beauty"
(trans. Cyril Scott. London: Elkin Mathews, 1909)

THE INNOCENT.
AN ENDANGERED SPECIES.
WHOSE FAULT WAS IT?
SMOKING KILLS
"SOMETIMES IT'S SIMPLY NOBODY'S FAULT."
Princess
DO YOU **REALLY** BELIEVE THAT?

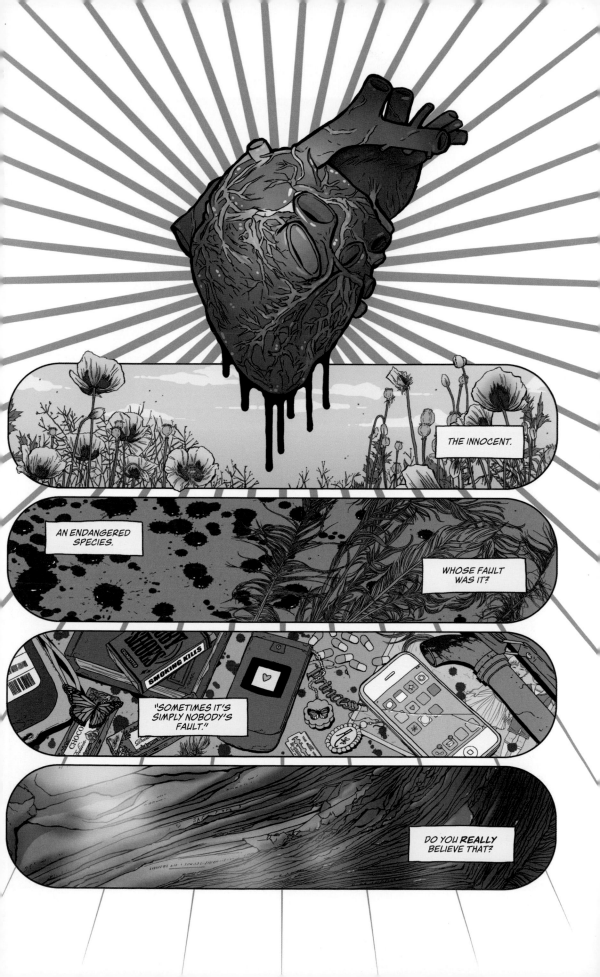

"IF THEY KEEP PUSHING YOU AGAIN AND AGAIN...
"...IS IT REALLY A SURPRISE IF YOU FINALLY RETURN THE BLOW?"
PRO CLEAN
PROZAC®
FLUOXETINE HYDROCHLORIDE
20 mg
10 mg
Temazepam Tablets
500 Tablets
MON
TUE
WED
THU
Clean
Pro Clean
Hospital
ANY EXCUSE IS A GOOD ONE WHEN ASSIGNING BLAME.

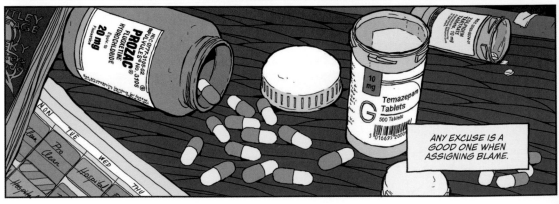

MOM...MOM, YOU HAVEN'T SIGNED THE SCHOLARSHIP FORMS.
ANEMONE GENETICS
ARMACY
BAR
HOTEL
DRUGS
MY BLOOD IS BLACK.
IT USED TO BE RED, GLEAMING, HYPNOTIC.
DRUGS

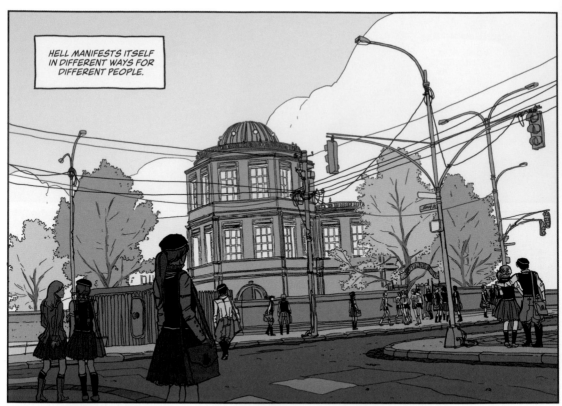

HELL MANIFESTS ITSELF IN DIFFERENT WAYS FOR DIFFERENT PEOPLE.

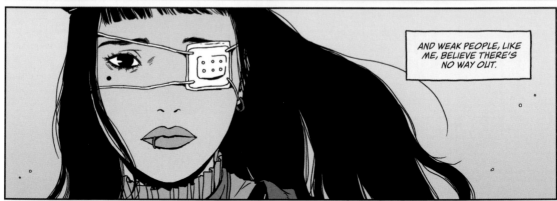

AND WEAK PEOPLE, LIKE ME, BELIEVE THERE'S NO WAY OUT.

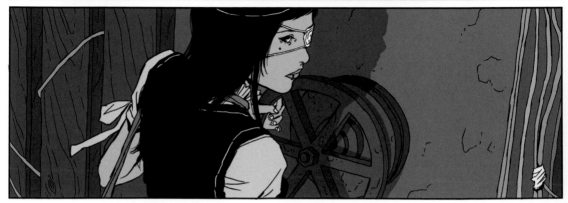

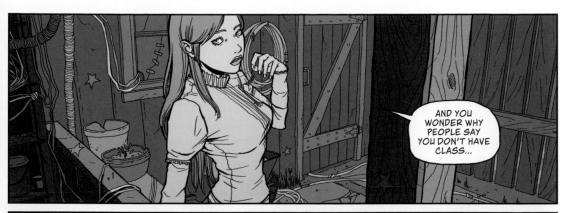

AND YOU WONDER WHY PEOPLE SAY YOU DON'T HAVE CLASS...

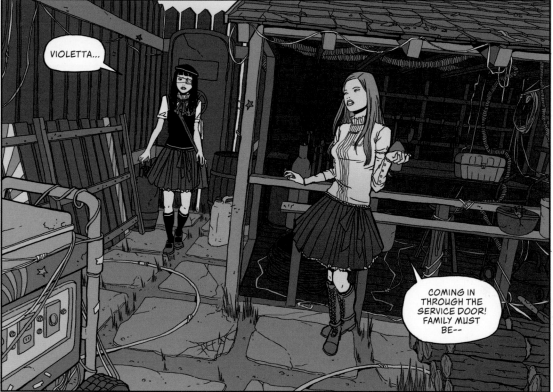

VIOLETTA...

COMING IN THROUGH THE SERVICE DOOR! FAMILY MUST BE--

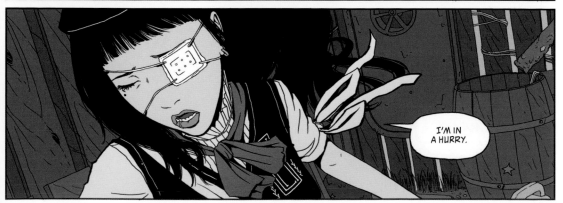

I'M IN A HURRY.

NOT A CHANCE!
EVEN WHEN THE EXIT APPEARS TO BE SO CLOSE...
MACK!

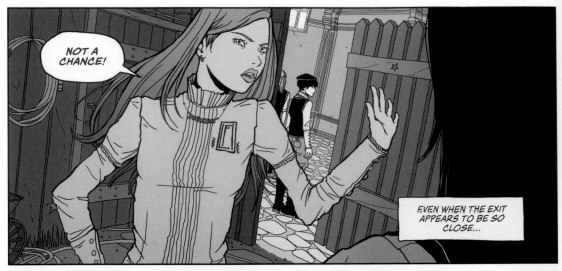

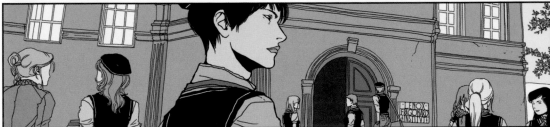

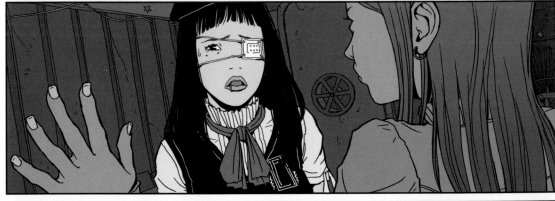

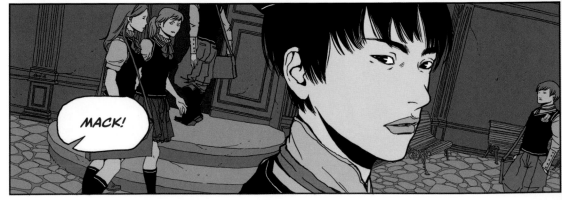

EVA! IT'S BEEN AGES!
HOW ARE YOU?
...
...
BREATHE!
HOW'S YOUR MOTHER?
GOOD... THANKS.
YOU DIDN'T HAPPEN TO SEE MY SISTER ON YOUR WAY IN, DID YOU?
NO.

I DON'T KNOW WHERE SHE WENT.
I THOUGHT YOU TWO WERE COMING TOGETHER.
NO...LATELY AMBER'S BEEN...
...OR SO FAR AWAY...

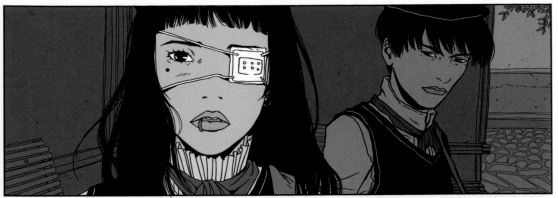

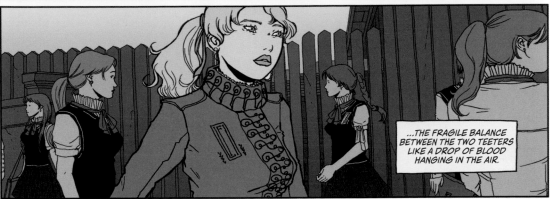

...THE FRAGILE BALANCE BETWEEN THE TWO TEETERS LIKE A DROP OF BLOOD HANGING IN THE AIR.

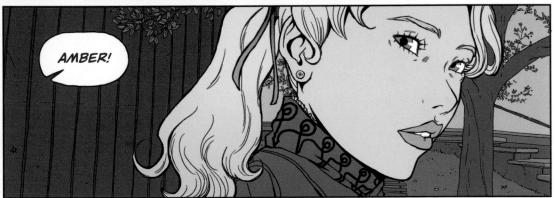

AMBER!

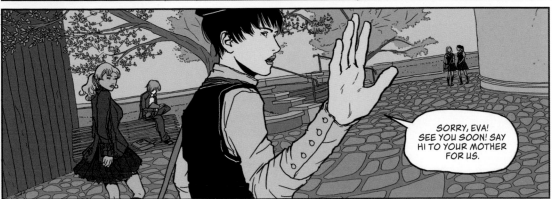

SORRY, EVA! SEE YOU SOON! SAY HI TO YOUR MOTHER FOR US.

WHERE WERE YOU? YOU LEFT YOUR HOMEWORK.
LEAVE ME ALONE.
AMBER...
LET GO OF ME! I TOLD YOU I WOULDN'T DO IT...
WELL, ONE OF US HAD TO.
...

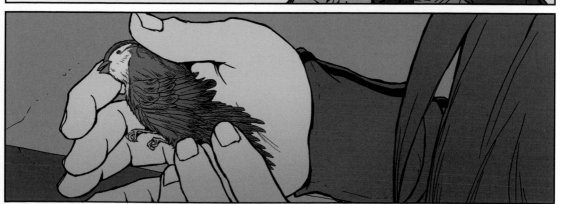

EVERYTHING AROUND US WAS A PURE FAÇADE...
♪ LET JUSTICE BE DONE THOUGH THE HEAVENS ♫ FALL.

♪ LET US SING TOGETHER WITH THE NEW DAY, LET US HOLD OUT A HAND AND SMILE. ♫

FIAT JUSTITIA RUAT CAELUM, LET US SING TOGETHER, OUR EDUCATION LIVES ON.
FIAT JUSTITIA RUAT CAELUM...
LET US SING TOGETHER UNTIL A NEW SUN RISES.
...CONCEALING OUR MOST DESPERATE LONGINGS.

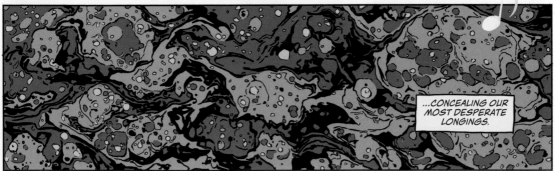

LOOKING BACK, IT WAS BECAUSE OF **BLOOD**. THERE CAN'T BE ANY OTHER REASON.
THERE WAS SO MUCH DESIRE IN ME...
...AND SO MUCH CONTEMPT SEEPING THROUGH MY PORES...
...CORRODING MY VEINS.
...
I'VE GOT THE SCHOLARSHIP FORMS.
LENOX FRAGONARD INSTITVTE
I SEE.

EW, WHAT COLOR IS THAT SHIRT?
IT'S THE SAME ONE SHE'S BEEN WEARING SINCE FRESHMAN YEAR!
HA HA HA
HERE YOU GO...
SINCE YOUR SCHOLARSHIP DOESN'T COVER ALL OF YOUR COSTS, REMIND YOUR MOTHER THAT PAYMENTS ARE DUE AT THE BEGINNING OF THE MONTH.
OKAY.

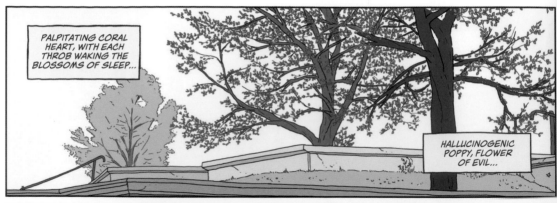

PALPITATING CORAL HEART, WITH EACH THROB WAKING THE BLOSSOMS OF SLEEP...

HALLUCINOGENIC POPPY, FLOWER OF EVIL...

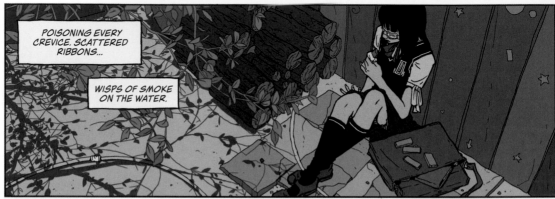

POISONING EVERY CREVICE. SCATTERED RIBBONS...

WISPS OF SMOKE ON THE WATER.

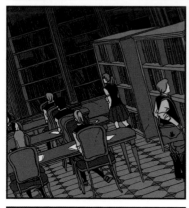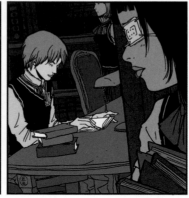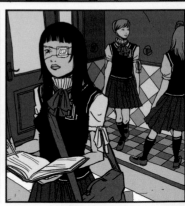

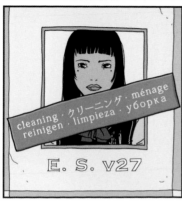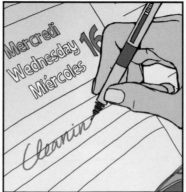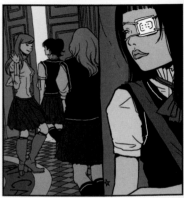

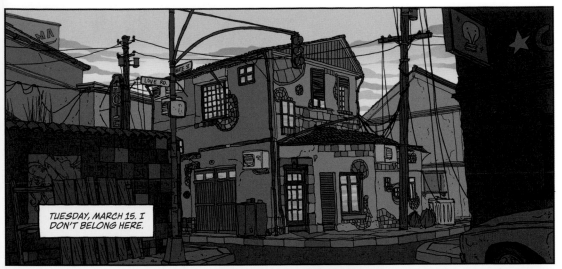

TUESDAY, MARCH 15. I DON'T BELONG HERE.

I KNOW IT. *EVERYBODY* KNOWS IT. EXCEPT MY MOTHER, OF COURSE. SHE'S THE ONLY ONE WHO DOESN'T UNDERSTAND.

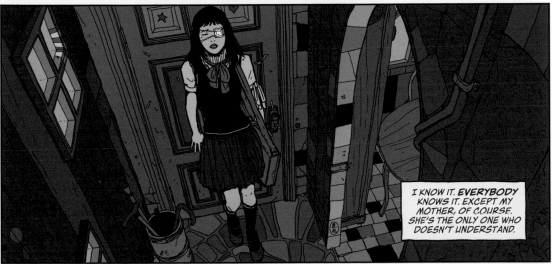

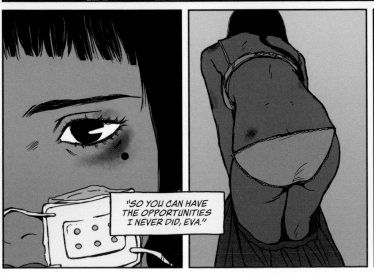

"SO YOU CAN HAVE THE OPPORTUNITIES I NEVER DID, EVA."

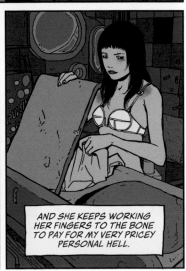

AND SHE KEEPS WORKING HER FINGERS TO THE BONE TO PAY FOR MY VERY PRICEY PERSONAL HELL.

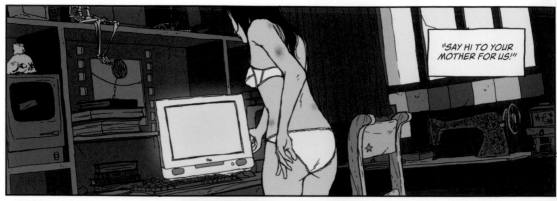

"SAY HI TO YOUR MOTHER FOR US!"

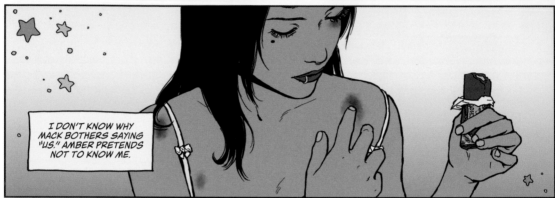

I DON'T KNOW WHY MACK BOTHERS SAYING "US." AMBER PRETENDS NOT TO KNOW ME.

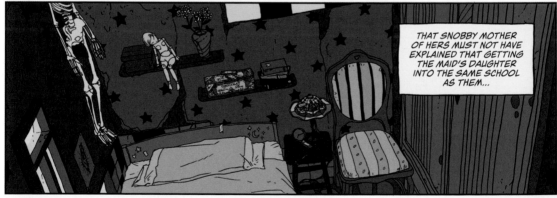

THAT SNOBBY MOTHER OF HERS MUST NOT HAVE EXPLAINED THAT GETTING THE MAID'S DAUGHTER INTO THE SAME SCHOOL AS THEM...

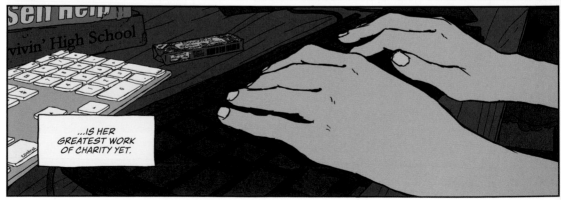

...IS HER GREATEST WORK OF CHARITY YET.

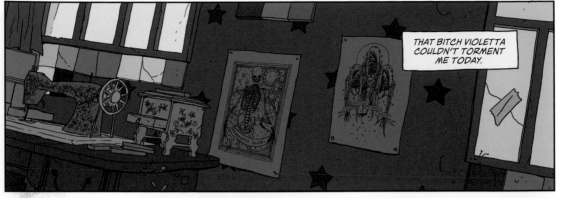

THAT BITCH VIOLETTA COULDN'T TORMENT ME TODAY.

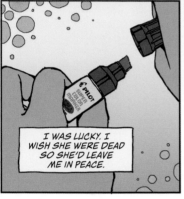

I WAS LUCKY. I WISH SHE WERE DEAD SO SHE'D LEAVE ME IN PEACE.

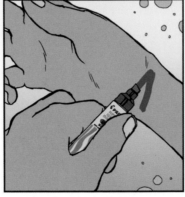

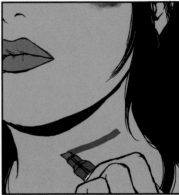

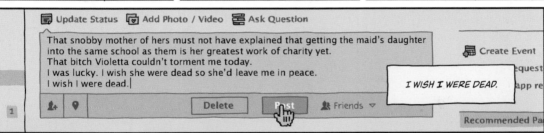

📋 Update Status 🖼 Add Photo / Video 🗐 Ask Question

That snobby mother of hers must not have explained that getting the maid's daughter into the same school as them is her greatest work of charity yet.
That bitch Violetta couldn't torment me today.
I was lucky. I wish she were dead so she'd leave me in peace.
I wish I were dead.

🚗 Create Event

...equest

...app re

I WISH I WERE DEAD.

👤+ 📍   Delete   Post 👥 Friends ▽

Recommended Pa...

1

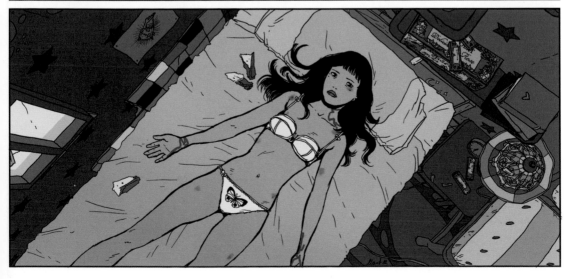

23

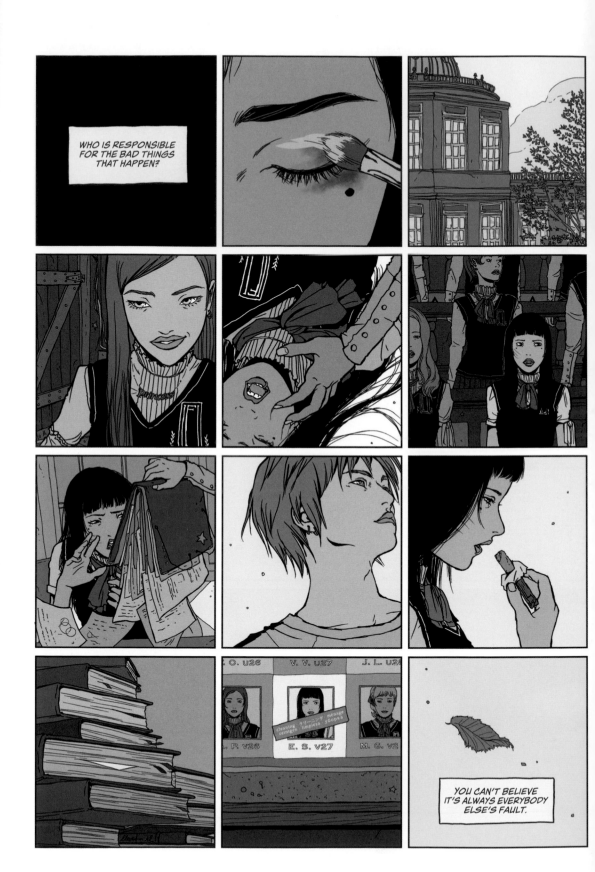

WHO IS RESPONSIBLE FOR THE BAD THINGS THAT HAPPEN?

YOU CAN'T BELIEVE IT'S ALWAYS EVERYBODY ELSE'S FAULT.

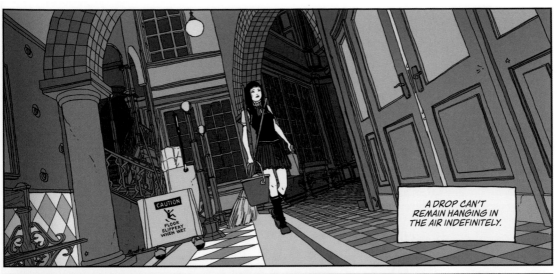

A DROP CAN'T REMAIN HANGING IN THE AIR INDEFINITELY.

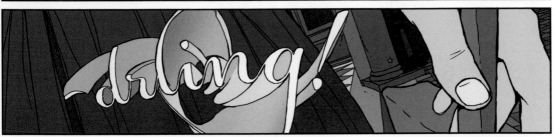

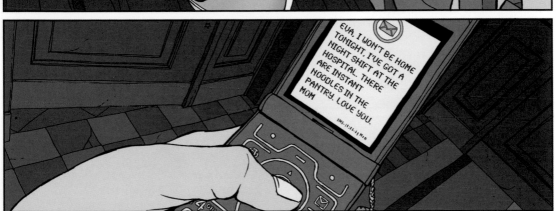

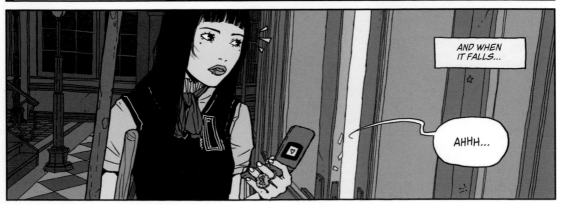

AND WHEN IT FALLS...

AHHH...

...IT BREAKS
THE BALANCE.

BLOOD...
BE EP!
AH!
CRASH!
CLONG!

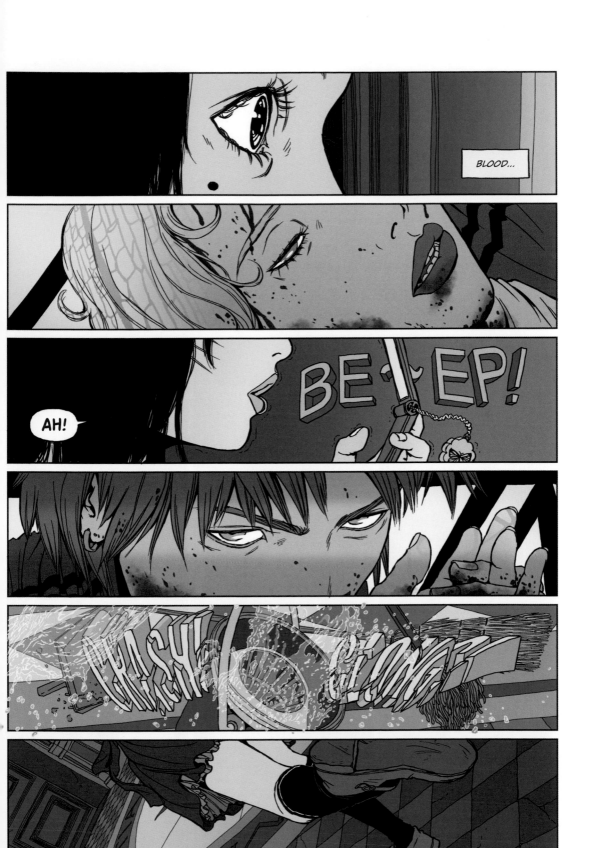

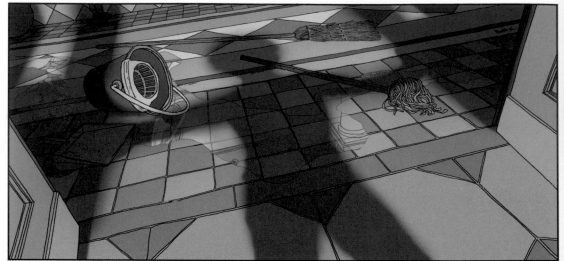

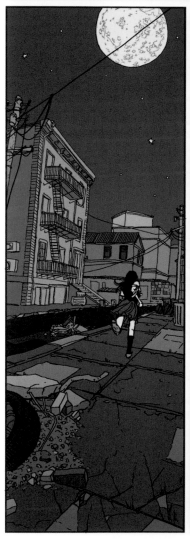

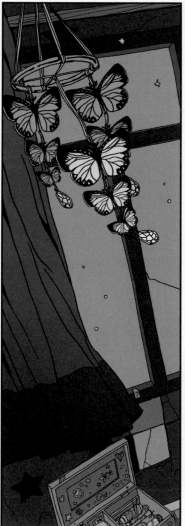

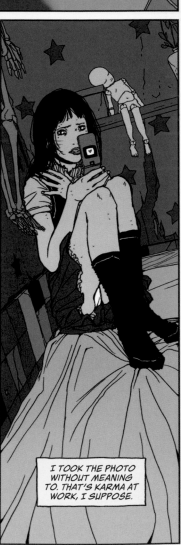

I TOOK THE PHOTO
WITHOUT MEANING
TO. THAT'S KARMA AT
WORK, I SUPPOSE.

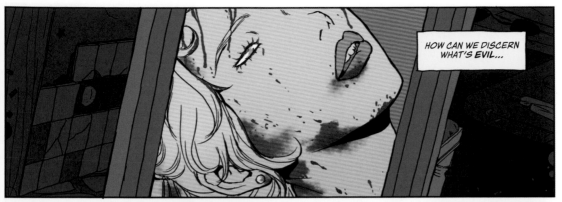

HOW CAN WE DISCERN WHAT'S **EVIL**...

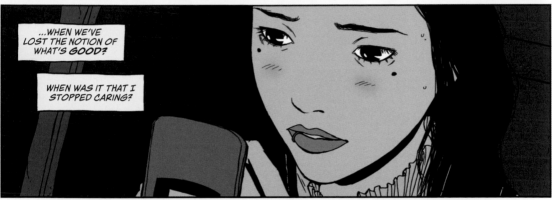

...WHEN WE'VE LOST THE NOTION OF WHAT'S **GOOD?**

WHEN WAS IT THAT I STOPPED CARING?

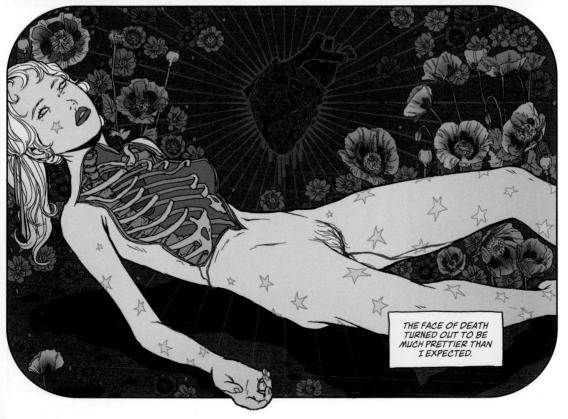

THE FACE OF DEATH TURNED OUT TO BE MUCH PRETTIER THAN I EXPECTED.

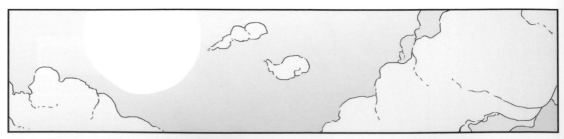

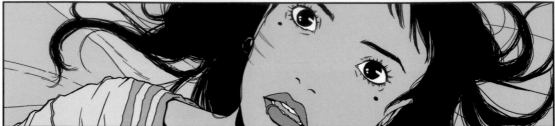

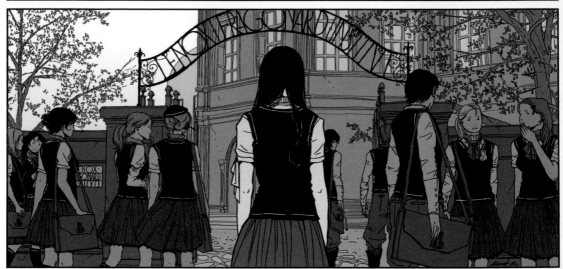

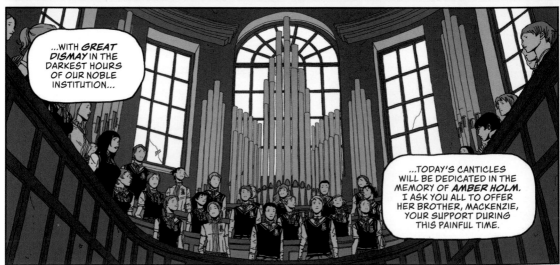

...WITH *GREAT DISMAY* IN THE DARKEST HOURS OF OUR NOBLE INSTITUTION...

...TODAY'S CANTICLES WILL BE DEDICATED IN THE MEMORY OF *AMBER HOLM.* I ASK YOU ALL TO OFFER HER BROTHER, MACKENZIE, YOUR SUPPORT DURING THIS PAINFUL TIME.

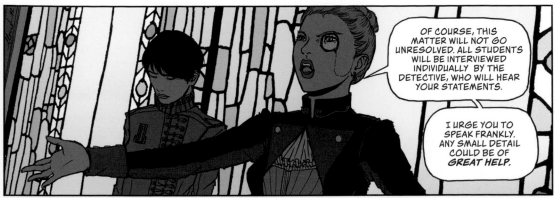

OF COURSE, THIS MATTER WILL NOT GO UNRESOLVED. ALL STUDENTS WILL BE INTERVIEWED INDIVIDUALLY BY THE DETECTIVE, WHO WILL HEAR YOUR STATEMENTS.

I URGE YOU TO SPEAK FRANKLY. ANY SMALL DETAIL COULD BE OF *GREAT HELP.*

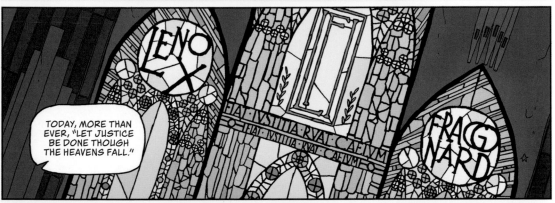

TODAY, MORE THAN EVER, "LET JUSTICE BE DONE THOUGH THE HEAVENS FALL."

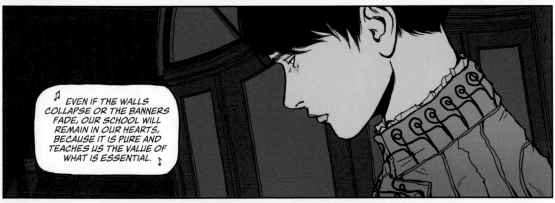

♪ EVEN IF THE WALLS COLLAPSE OR THE BANNERS FADE, OUR SCHOOL WILL REMAIN IN OUR HEARTS, BECAUSE IT IS PURE AND TEACHES US THE VALUE OF WHAT IS ESSENTIAL. ♪

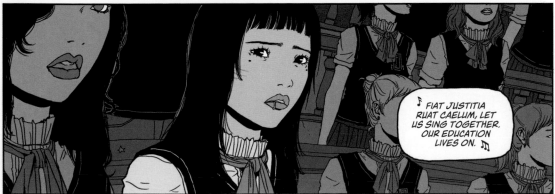

♪ FIAT JUSTITIA RUAT CAELUM, LET US SING TOGETHER. OUR EDUCATION LIVES ON. ♪♪

FIAT JUSTITIA RUAT CAELUM, LET US SING TOGETHER UNTIL THE END OF TIMES.
YOU CAN'T THINK YOU'RE INNOCENT.
IS THERE ANYTHING ELSE YOU WANT TO ADD? SOMETHING YOU'VE SEEN OR HEARD?
NO.

NO.
NO.
NO.
...

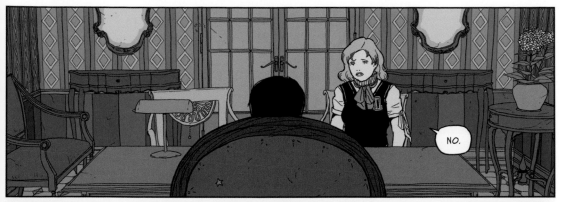

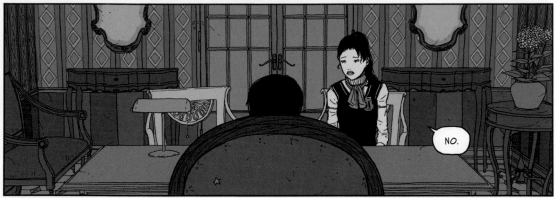

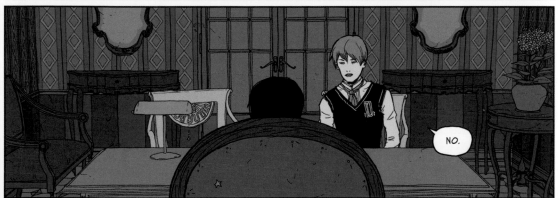

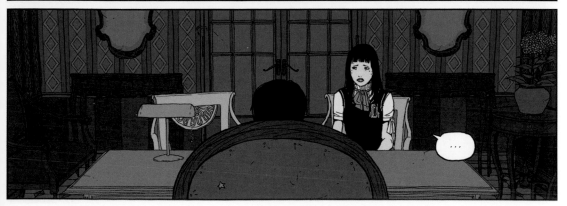

NO.
ALL RIGHT. IF YOU THINK OF ANYTHING YOU WANT TO TELL ME, YOU CAN CALL THIS NUMBER.
ANYTHING YOU SAY WILL BE HELD IN STRICTEST CONFIDENCE, OF COURSE.
DETECTIVE R.
602 555 0146

...THANK YOU.
MACK...I'M SORRY...
HYPOCRITE.
I APPRECIATE YOUR SUPPORT, EVA.
SORRY FOR YOUR LOSS.

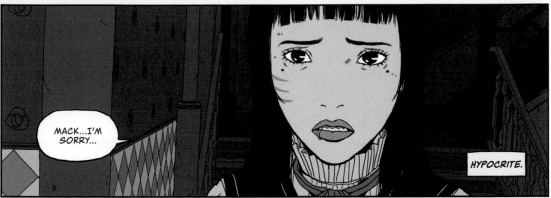

BASTARD!
I'LL KILL YOU!

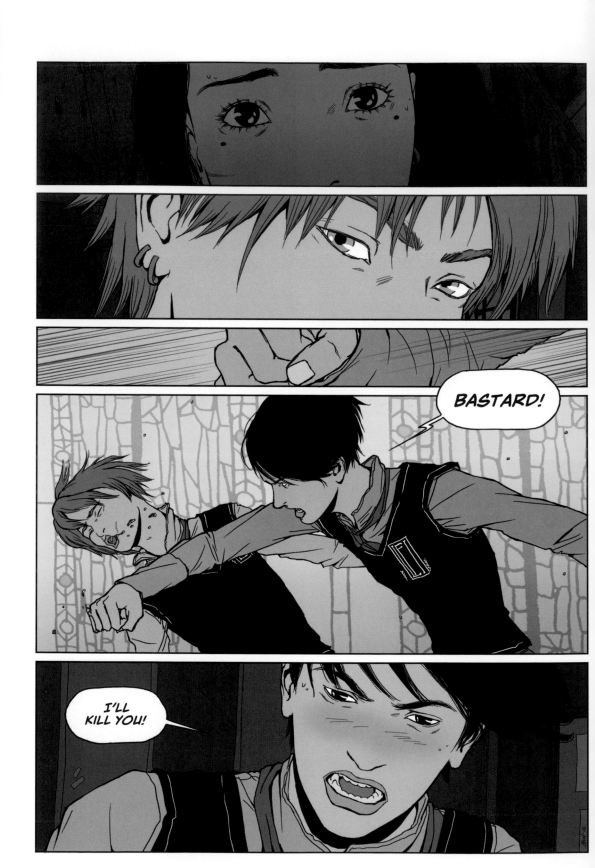

I KNOW IT WAS YOU, ASSHOLE!
MACK! CALM DOWN!
THURSDAY, MARCH 17. DONATIEN SAW ME LEAVING THE CHORUS ROOM.

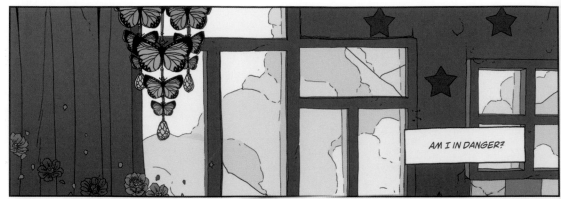

AM I IN DANGER?

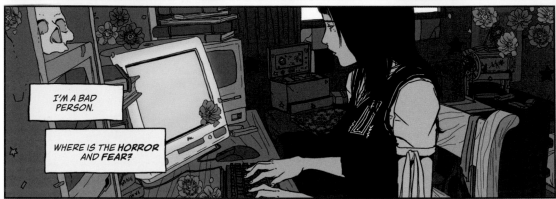

I'M A BAD PERSON.

WHERE IS THE HORROR AND FEAR?

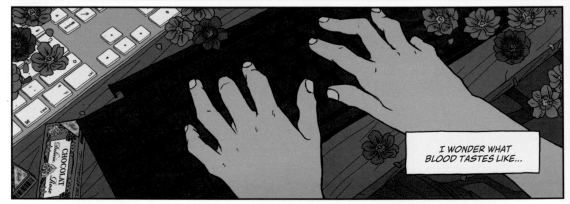

I WONDER WHAT BLOOD TASTES LIKE...

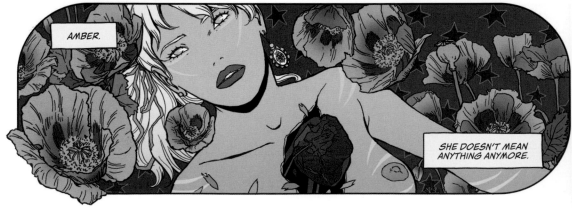

AMBER.

SHE DOESN'T MEAN ANYTHING ANYMORE.

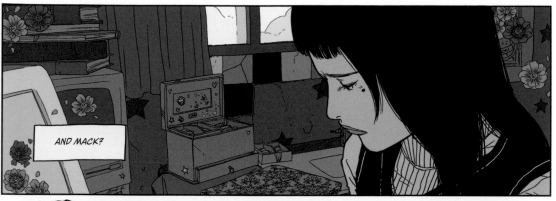

AND MACK?

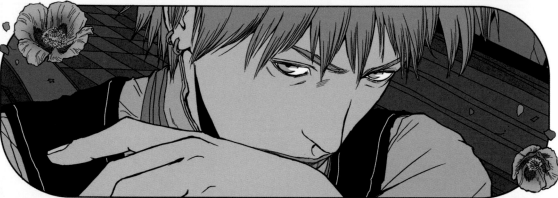

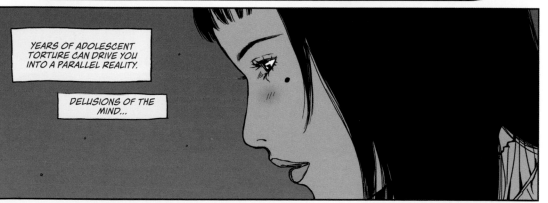

YEARS OF ADOLESCENT
TORTURE CAN DRIVE YOU
INTO A PARALLEL REALITY.

DELUSIONS OF THE
MIND...

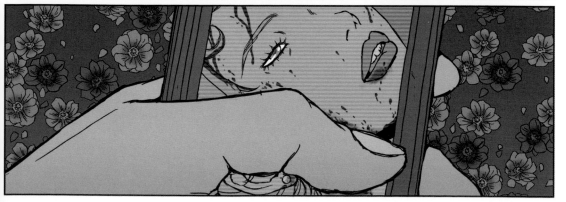

...WHICH SEES WHAT IT WANTS TO SEE...
EVA.
...WHERE THERE IS ONLY THE VEIL OF A SHADOW, REFLECTED ON RAYS OF LIGHT AND FLECKS OF SKY.

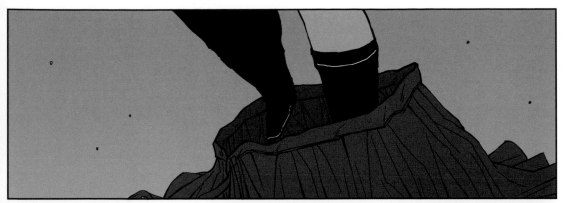

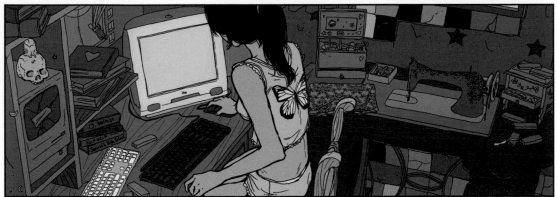

Amber. She doesn't mean anything anymore.
And Mack...?|

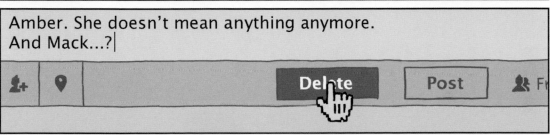

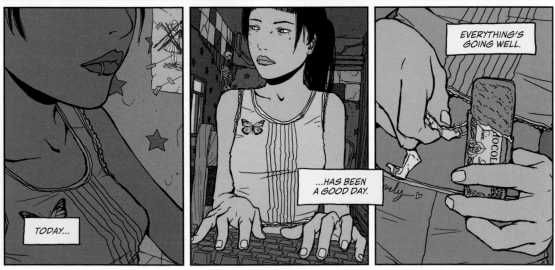

TODAY...

...HAS BEEN A GOOD DAY.

EVERYTHING'S GOING WELL.

Delete
Post
Friends

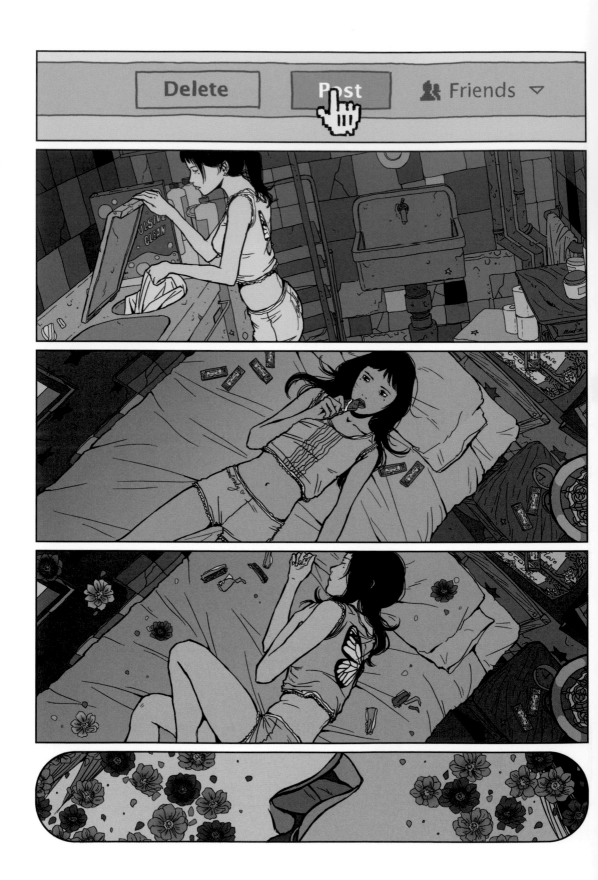

43

AHH! GROSS!
KILL IT!
NO!
DON'T YOU SEE IT'S A WORM? IT'S GROSS LIKE YOU!

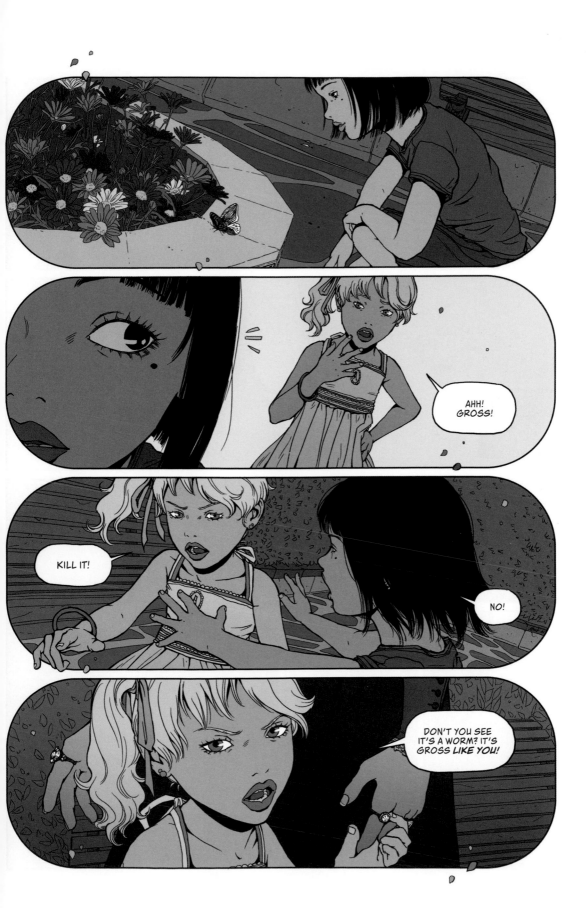

DID YOU MISS ME?
WE CREATE OUR OWN ENEMIES.
WHY DO YOU KEEP HITTING WHEN I'M ALREADY DOWN?

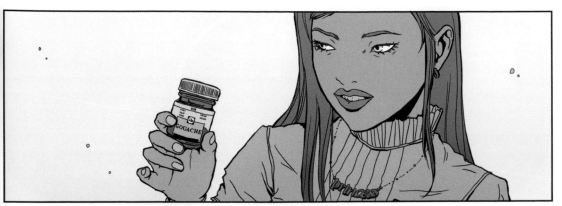

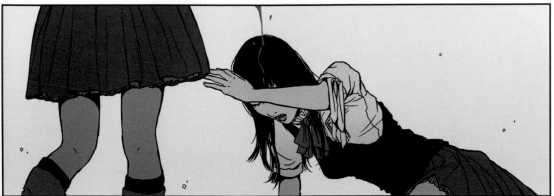

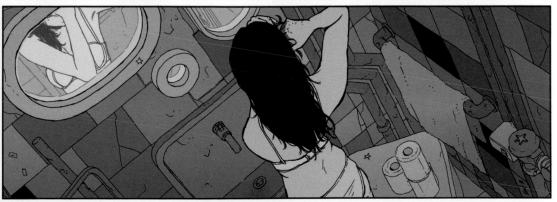

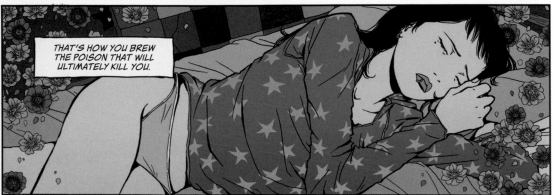

THAT'S HOW YOU BREW
THE POISON THAT WILL
ULTIMATELY KILL YOU.

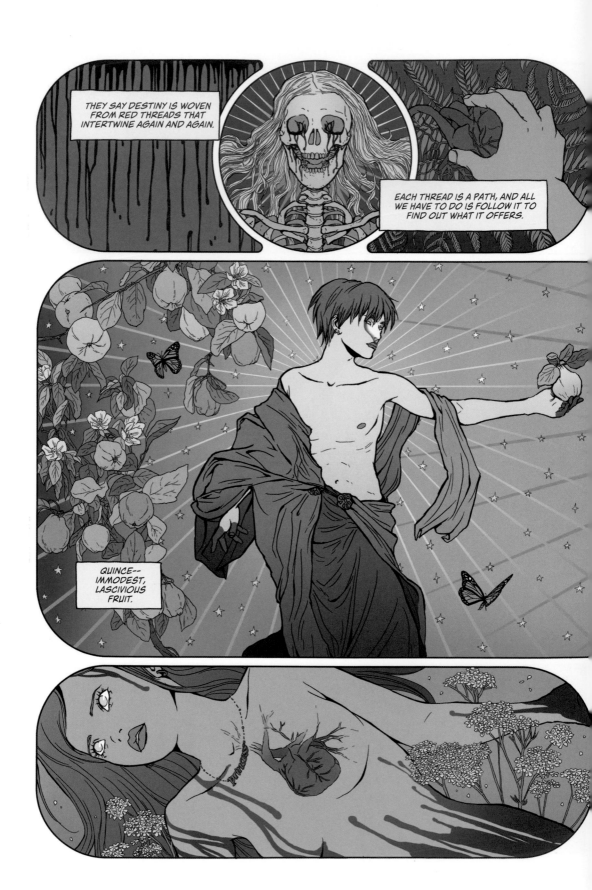

THEY SAY DESTINY IS WOVEN FROM RED THREADS THAT INTERTWINE AGAIN AND AGAIN.

EACH THREAD IS A PATH, AND ALL WE HAVE TO DO IS FOLLOW IT TO FIND OUT WHAT IT OFFERS.

QUINCE-- IMMODEST, LASCIVIOUS FRUIT.

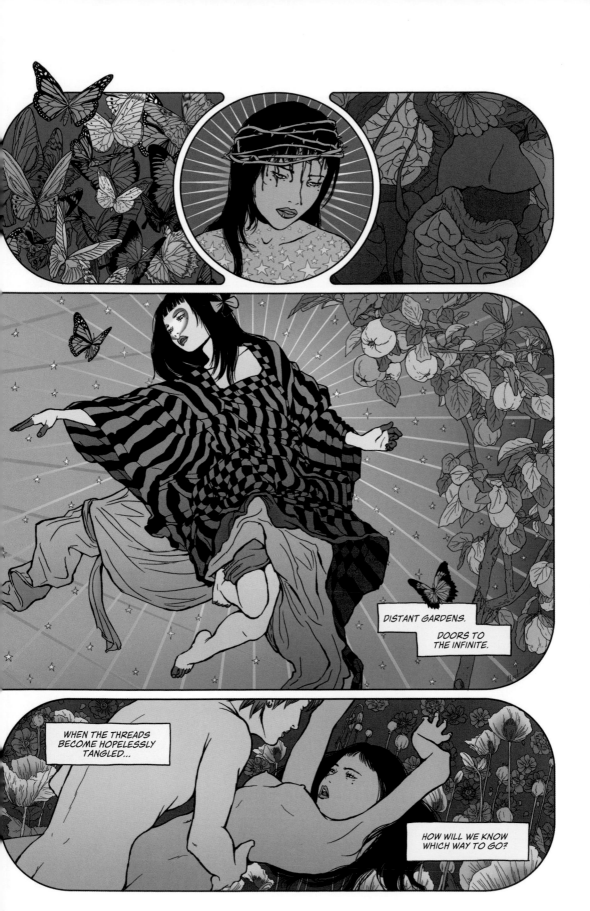

DISTANT GARDENS.

DOORS TO
THE INFINITE.

WHEN THE THREADS
BECOME HOPELESSLY
TANGLED...

HOW WILL WE KNOW
WHICH WAY TO GO?

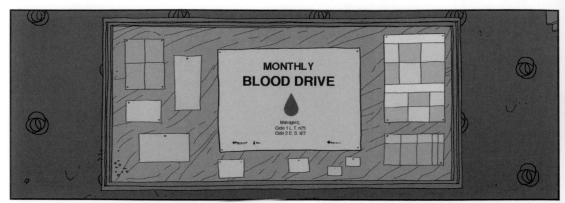

MONTHLY
BLOOD DRIVE

Managers;
Odo 1 L. T. n75
Odo 2 E. S. \27

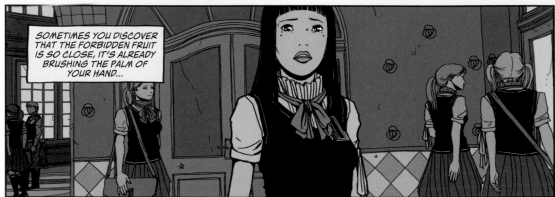

SOMETIMES YOU DISCOVER THAT THE FORBIDDEN FRUIT IS SO CLOSE, IT'S ALREADY BRUSHING THE PALM OF YOUR HAND...

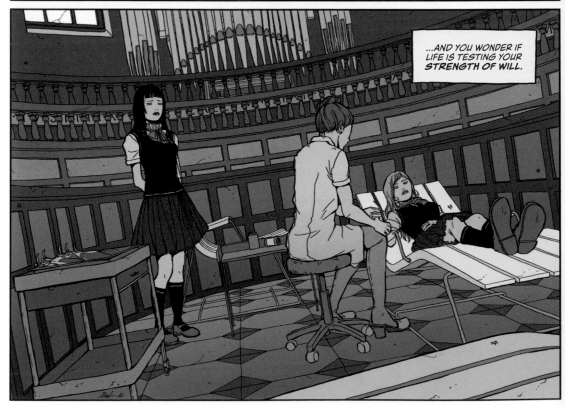

...AND YOU WONDER IF LIFE IS TESTING YOUR **STRENGTH OF WILL.**

2362
B
2363
B
2364
A

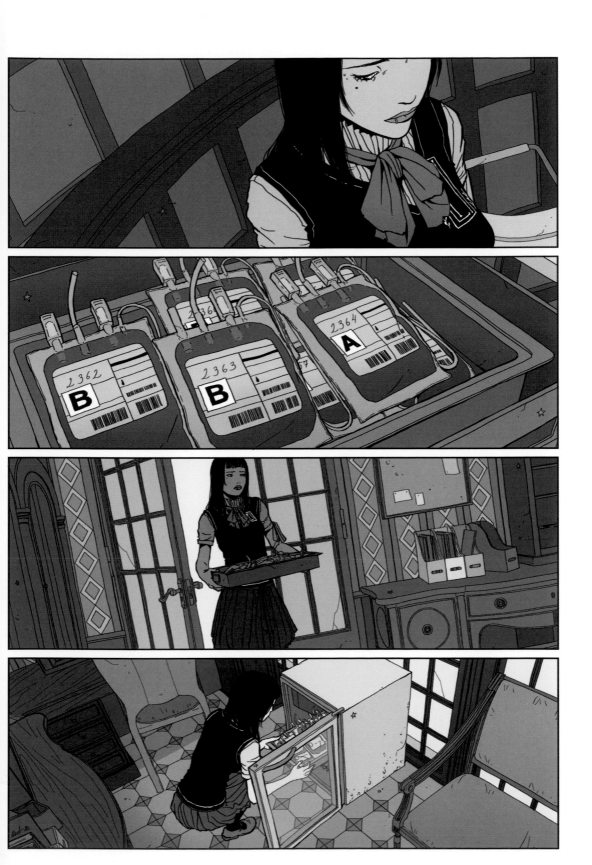

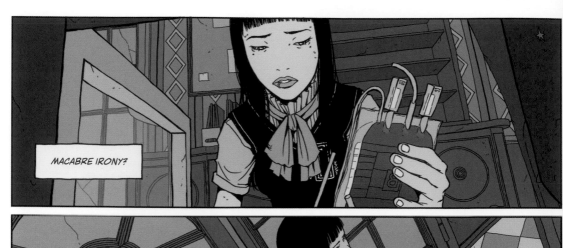

MACABRE IRONY?

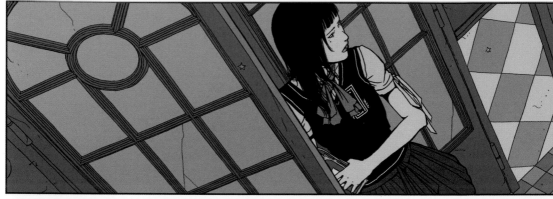

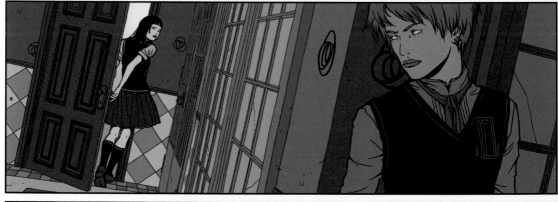

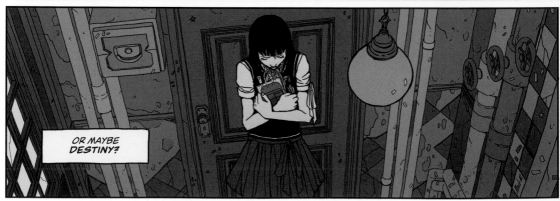

OR MAYBE
DESTINY?

2362
B
REGRETS?
WHAT GOOD ARE THEY
ONCE IT'S TOO LATE?

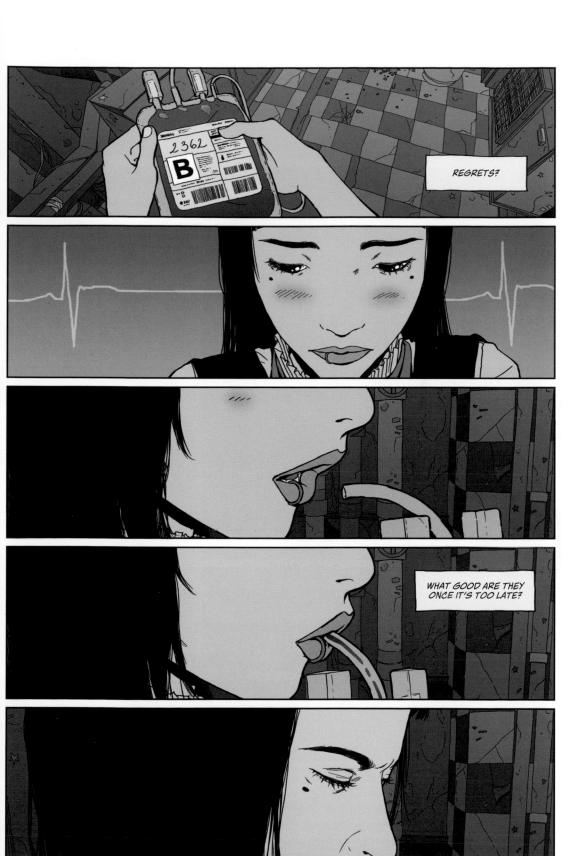

Splat!
COUGH
COUGH
COUGH
COUGH
I WALKED THROUGH SO MANY DOORS.
BUT WHAT NOBODY SEEMS TO UNDERSTAND...

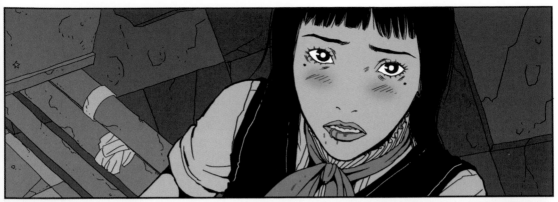

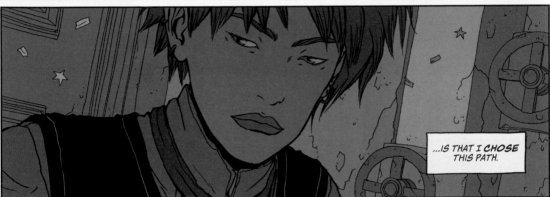

...IS THAT I **CHOSE** THIS PATH.

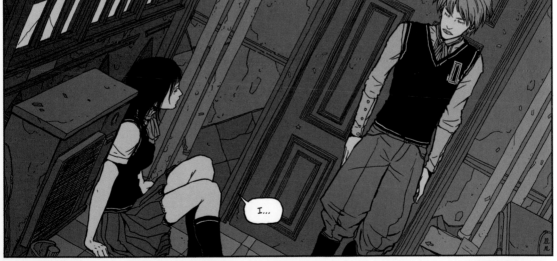

I...

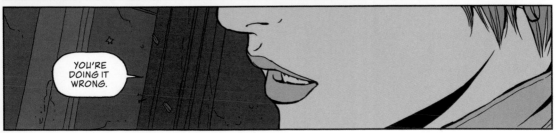

YOU'RE DOING IT WRONG.

SHOW ME?
I COULD HAVE TURNED BACK AT ANY MOMENT...

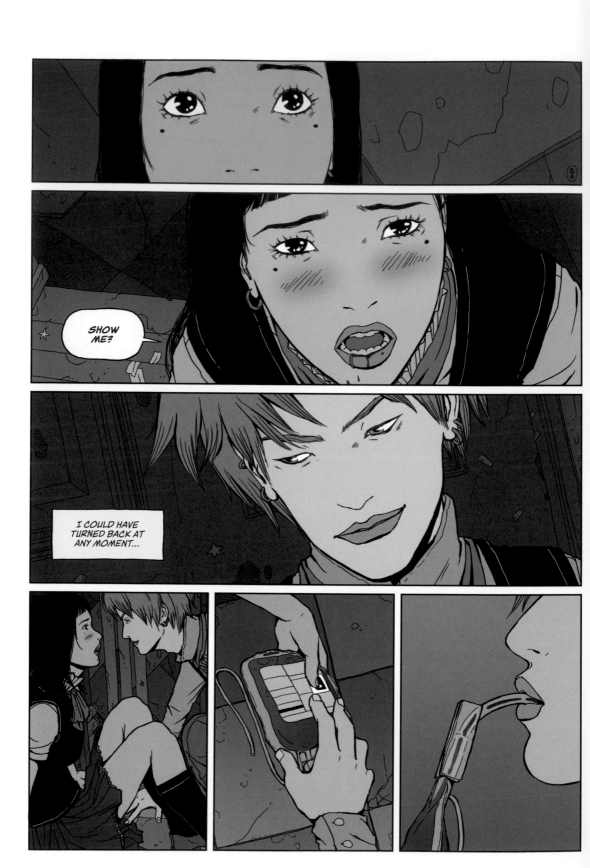

AND YET...

DETECTIVE
602 555 0146

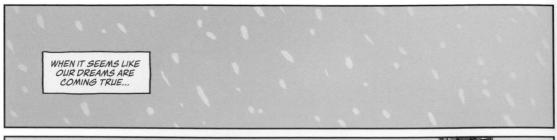

WHEN IT SEEMS LIKE
OUR DREAMS ARE
COMING TRUE...

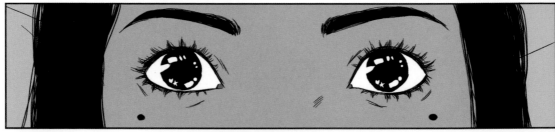

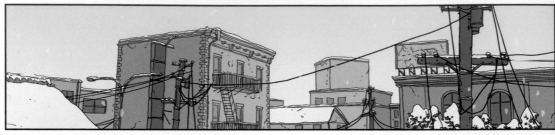

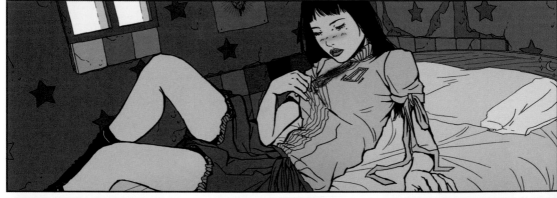

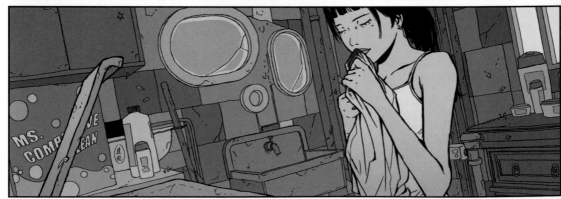

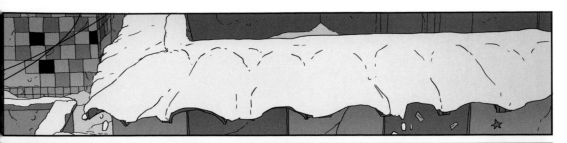

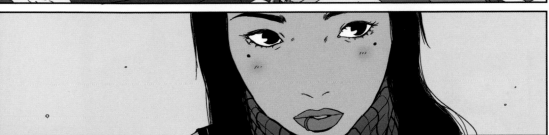

...WE MUST ASK WHAT PRICE WE'LL PAY WHEN WE **WAKE UP.**

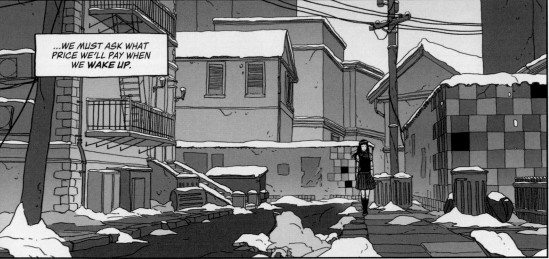

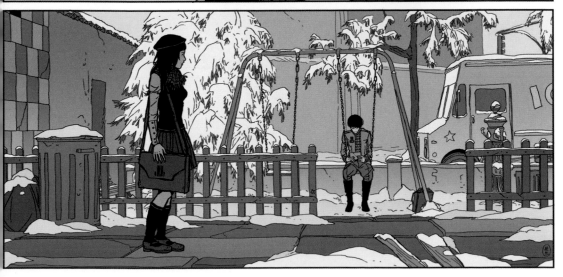

HEY.
HEY.
DO YOU REMEMBER THOSE DAYS?
NOT REALLY...
LIES.

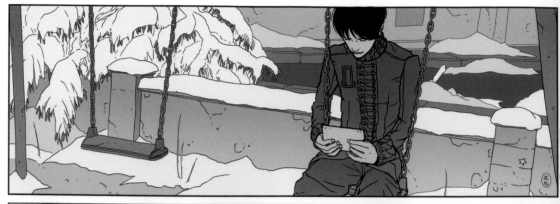

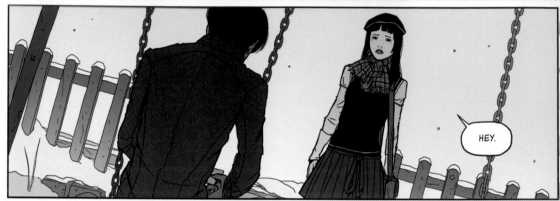

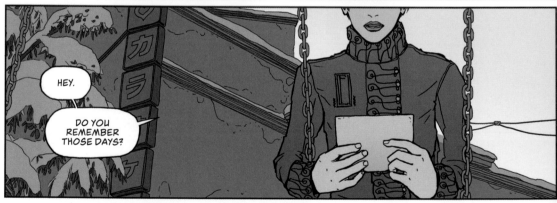

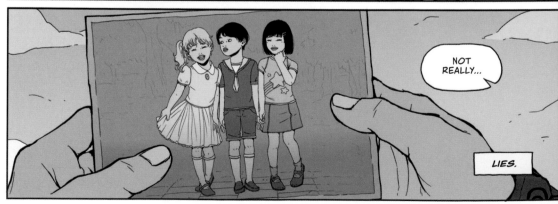

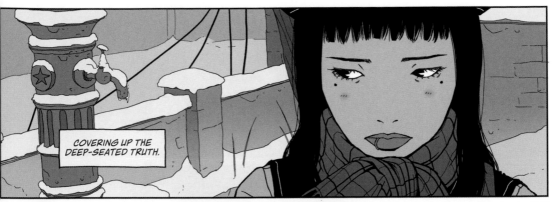

COVERING UP THE DEEP-SEATED TRUTH.

HOW ARE YOU, MACK?

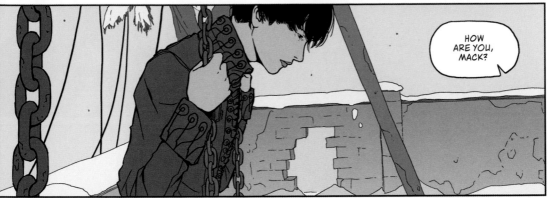

I DON'T KNOW... I DON'T THINK I'VE PROCESSED THAT I'VE LOST HER...

IT'S HIT MY MOTHER HARDER. SHE DIDN'T EVEN GO TO THE FUNERAL.

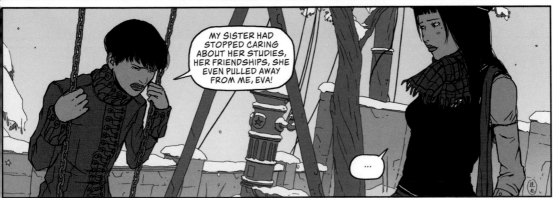

MY SISTER HAD STOPPED CARING ABOUT HER STUDIES, HER FRIENDSHIPS, SHE EVEN PULLED AWAY FROM ME, EVA!

...

61

SHE WASN'T HERSELF ANYMORE...MY AMBER...
BECAUSE OF HIM!
MACK... THINGS LIKE THIS HAPPEN AS WE GROW UP...
I KNOW...BUT EVEN IF NOBODY BELIEVES ME...

I KNOW IT WAS HIM...AND I'LL FIND A WAY TO PROVE IT...
...IF IT'S THE LAST THING I DO.
MACK...
WE'RE GOING TO BE LATE.

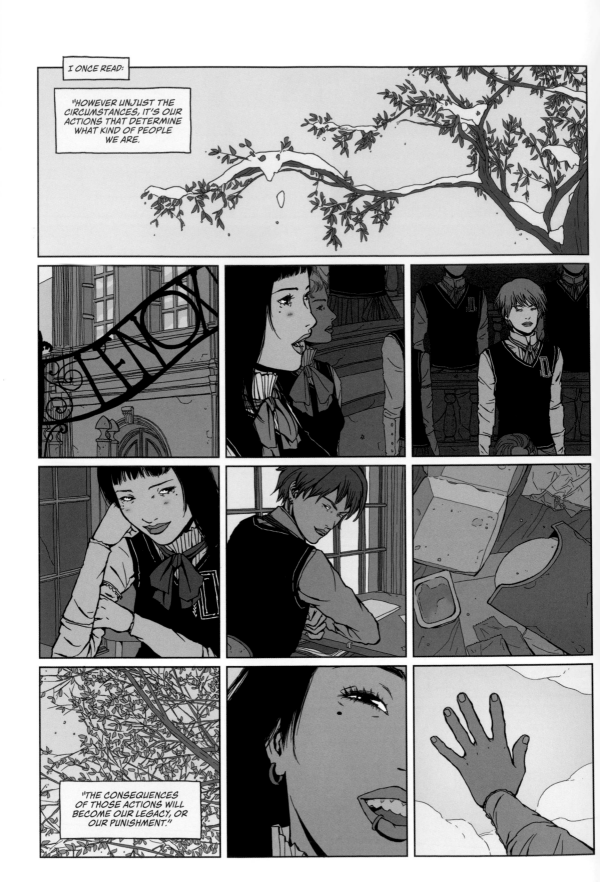

I ONCE READ:

"HOWEVER UNJUST THE CIRCUMSTANCES, IT'S OUR ACTIONS THAT DETERMINE WHAT KIND OF PEOPLE WE ARE.

"THE CONSEQUENCES OF THOSE ACTIONS WILL BECOME OUR LEGACY, OR OUR PUNISHMENT."

...

OH...

DONATIEN...
SO SOFT...
MMM...
I WANT... TO TASTE IT AGAIN.
TONIGHT YOU'LL STAY AT MY HOUSE.

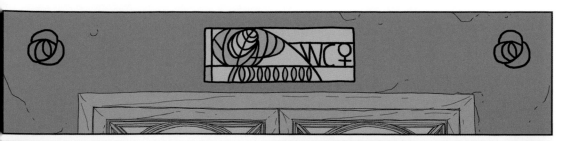

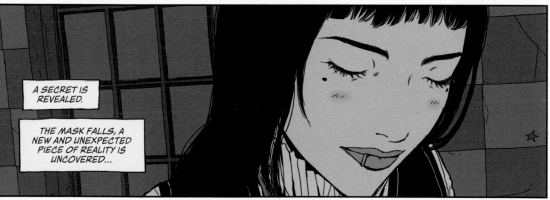

A SECRET IS
REVEALED.

THE MASK FALLS, A
NEW AND UNEXPECTED
PIECE OF REALITY IS
UNCOVERED...

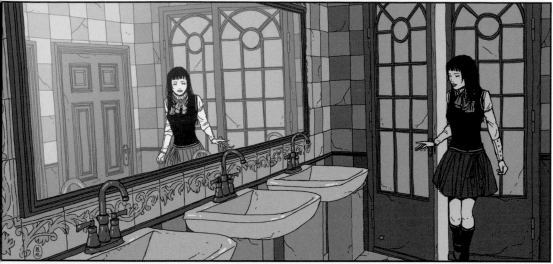

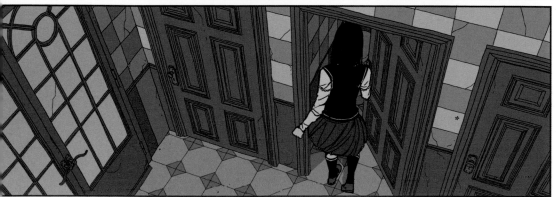

PLEASE, DAD, LISTEN TO ME...
NO!
DAD...PLEASE... YOU CAN'T DECIDE THIS ON YOUR OWN!
BITCH
CAN'T WE AT LEAST TALK?
NO! DON'T YOU GET IT? IT'S MY FUTURE!
DAD...I KNOW, BUT...I'VE TRIED TO TELL YOU A MILLION TIMES AND--
NO! YOU KNEW PERFECTLY WELL...
NO!
DAD, WAIT, PLEASE! DAD...?
FUCK!

I'M **NOT** YOUR FUCKING PRINCESS!
...AND A BIT OF LIGHT GIVES ORDER TO CHAOS.
sob

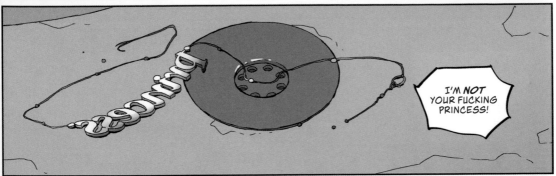

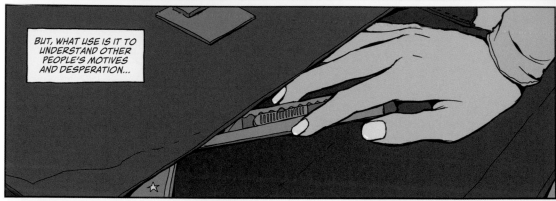

BUT, WHAT USE IS IT TO UNDERSTAND OTHER PEOPLE'S MOTIVES AND DESPERATION...

...WHEN YOU CAN'T UNDERSTAND YOUR OWN?

OR, ARE THEY THE SAME THING?
EVA...
WITHOUT THE EVILS THAT FOSTER THEIR ANXIETIES, WOULD THEY PROVOKE YOUR OWN?

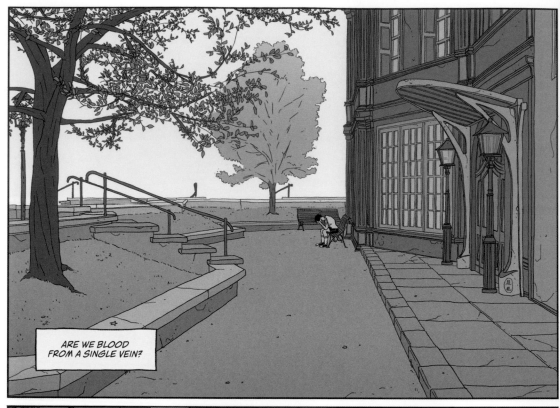

ARE WE BLOOD
FROM A SINGLE VEIN?

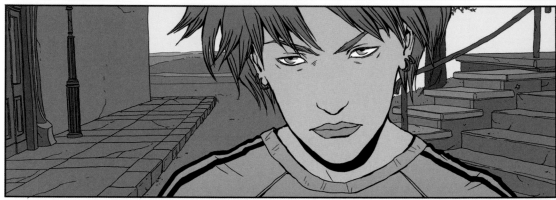

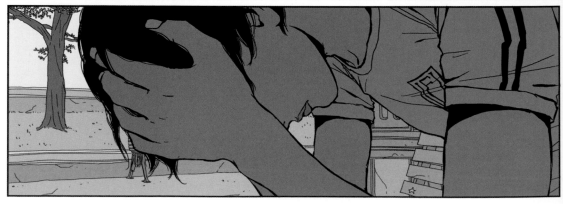

YOU!
TOUCH ME AGAIN AND I'LL KILL YOU.
...
SHAME ABOUT YOUR SISTER...WHO ARE YOU GOING TO HARASS NOW?
WHAT THE HELL ARE YOU TALKING ABOUT?

AMBER TOLD ME EVERYTHING, MORON.
YOU KNOW, I THINK THAT DETECTIVE, AND ESPECIALLY YOUR MOTHER, WOULD BE VERY INTERESTED IN THOSE *TENDENCIES* OF YOURS...
PERVERT.
SON OF A BITCH...
IF YOU'VE SPRINKLED THE GASOLINE, LIT THE MATCH, AND FED THE FLAME...

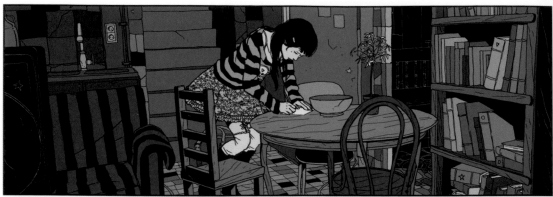

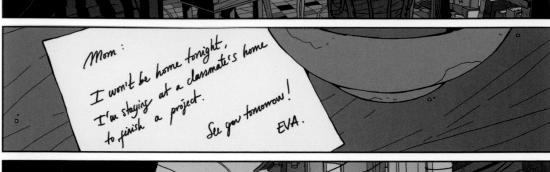

Mom:

I won't be home tonight,
I'm staying at a classmate's home
to finish a project.

See you tomorrow!

EVA.

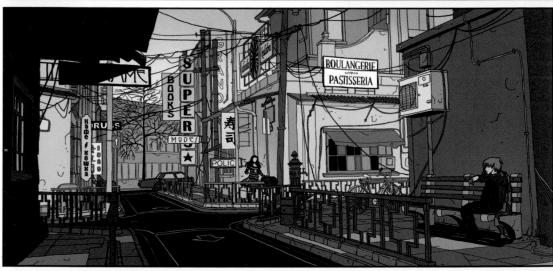

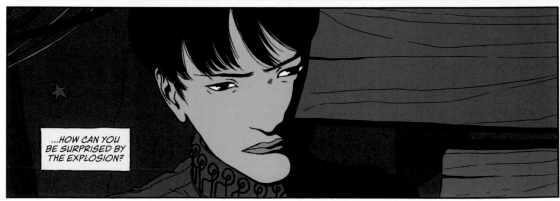

...HOW CAN YOU
BE SURPRISED BY
THE EXPLOSION?

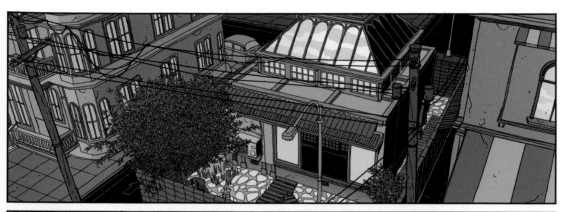

WHOA!

THE
SUBTLETIES.

78

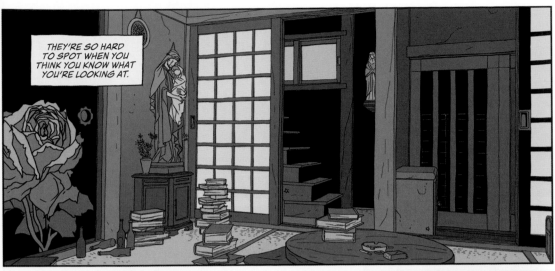

THEY'RE SO HARD TO SPOT WHEN YOU THINK YOU KNOW WHAT YOU'RE LOOKING AT.

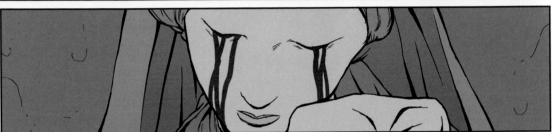

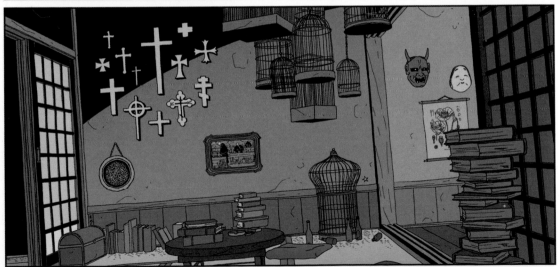

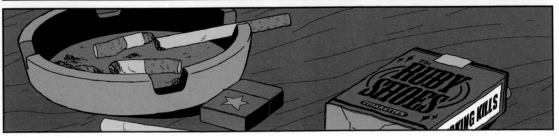

COME.

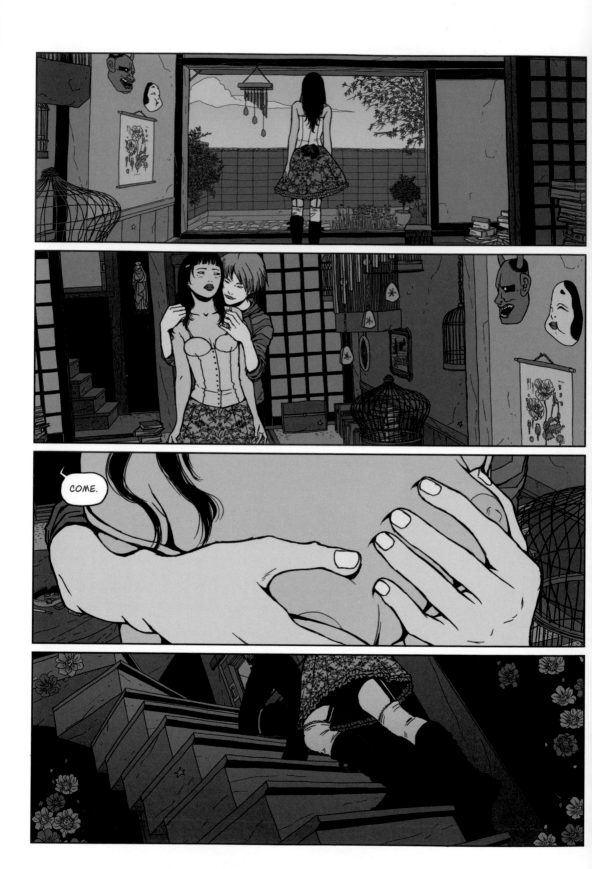

AH....!

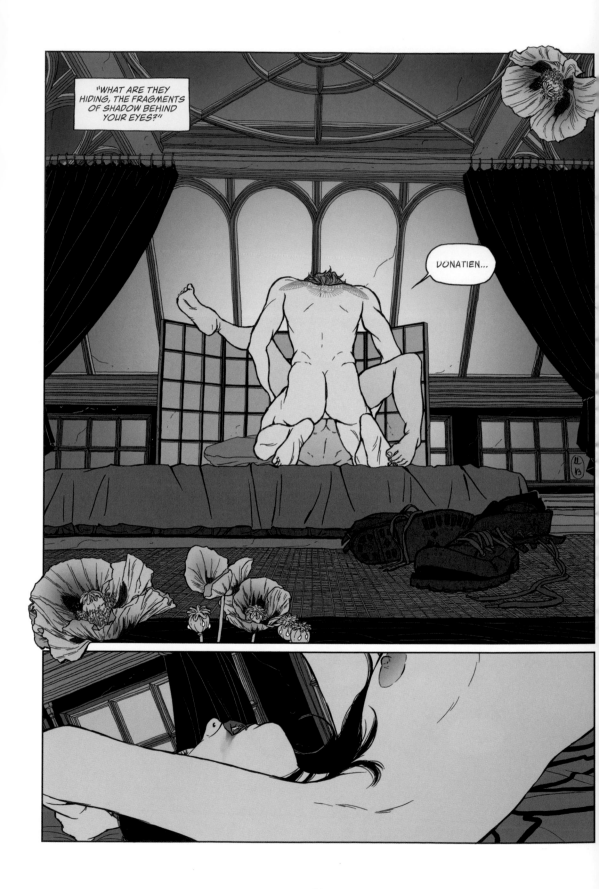

"WHAT ARE THEY HIDING, THE FRAGMENTS OF SHADOW BEHIND YOUR EYES?"

DONATIEN...

82

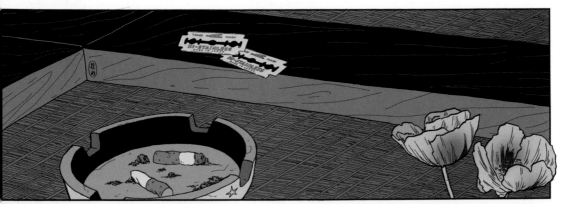

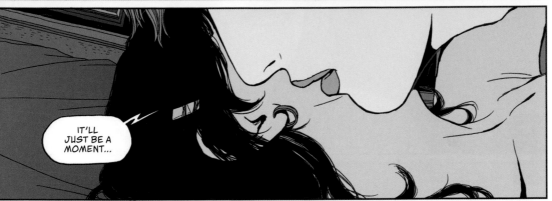

IT'LL JUST BE A MOMENT...

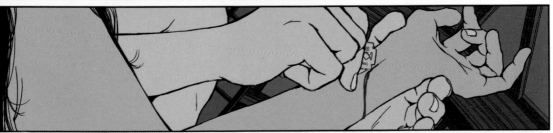

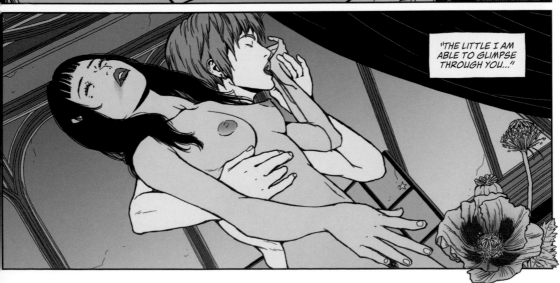

"THE LITTLE I AM ABLE TO GLIMPSE THROUGH YOU..."

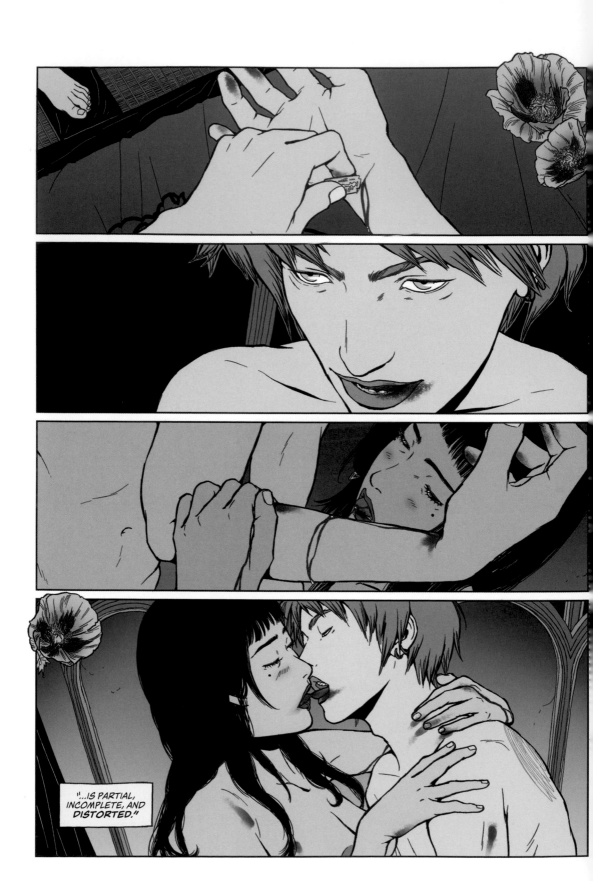

"...IS PARTIAL, INCOMPLETE, AND DISTORTED."

HOTEL

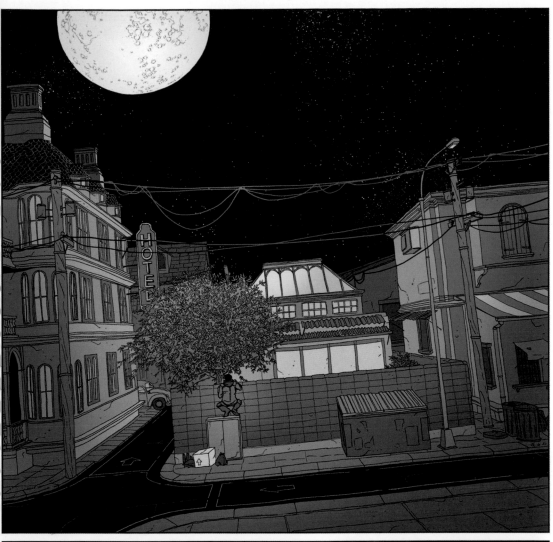

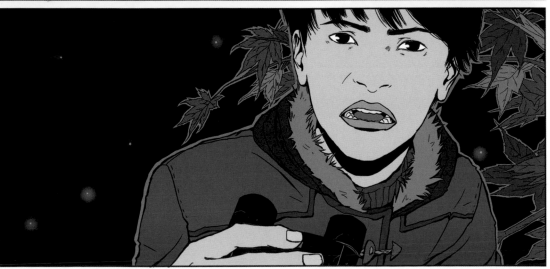

WHAT WAS IT LIKE?
THERE'S NO WAY I CAN DESCRIBE--
HER HEARTBEAT...IT WAS POUNDING SO *LOUD...*
I WANTED TO TOUCH IT WITH MY OWN HANDS...

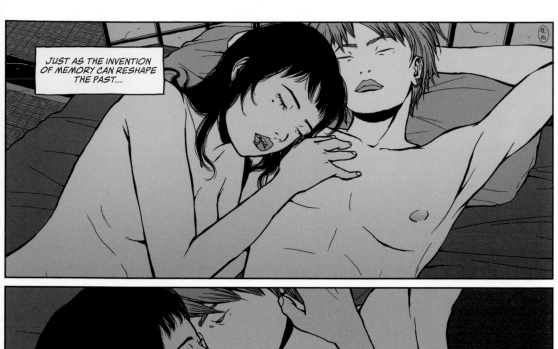

JUST AS THE INVENTION OF MEMORY CAN RESHAPE THE PAST...

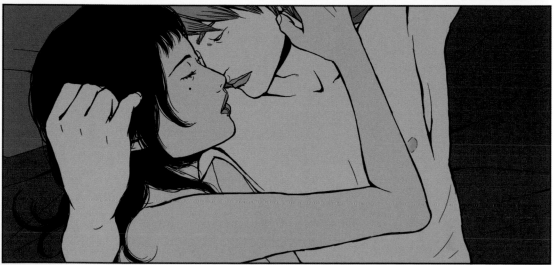

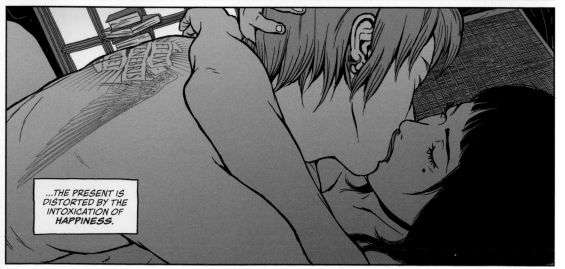

...THE PRESENT IS DISTORTED BY THE INTOXICATION OF **HAPPINESS.**

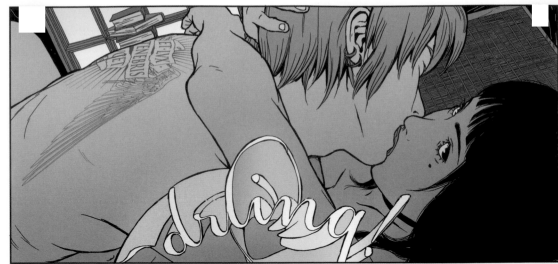

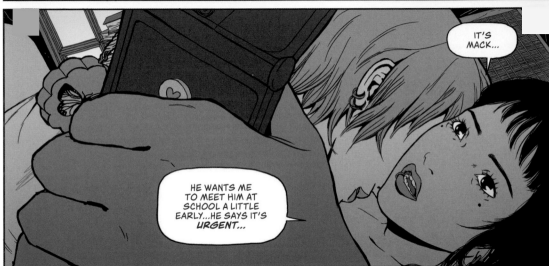

IT'S MACK...

HE WANTS ME TO MEET HIM AT SCHOOL A LITTLE EARLY...HE SAYS IT'S *URGENT*...

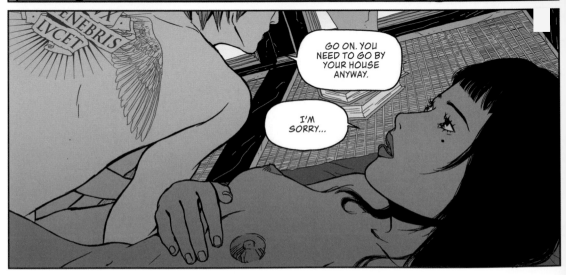

GO ON. YOU NEED TO GO BY YOUR HOUSE ANYWAY.

I'M SORRY...

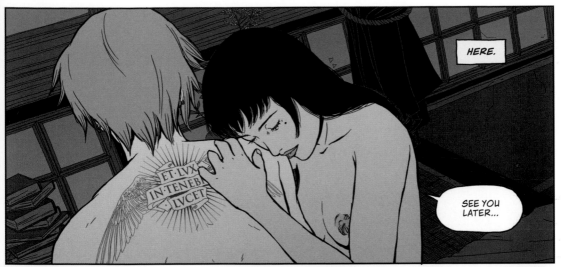

HERE.

SEE YOU LATER...

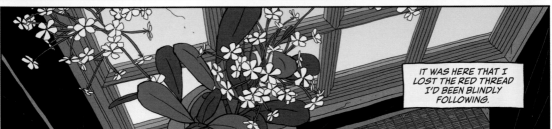

IT WAS HERE THAT I LOST THE RED THREAD I'D BEEN BLINDLY FOLLOWING.

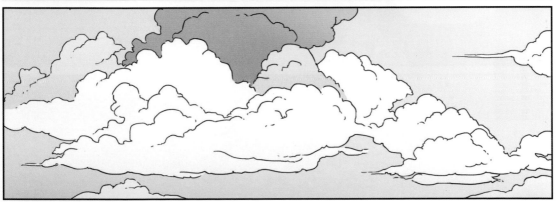

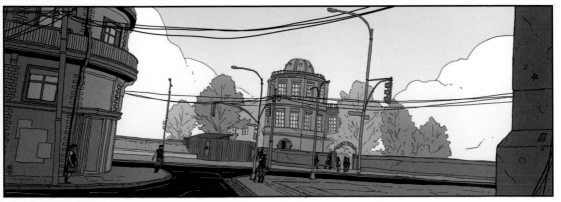

LENOX FRAGONARD INSTITUTE
EVA!
FINALLY! I THOUGHT...
CAN WE TALK SOMEWHERE A LITTLE MORE PRIVATE?
WHAT'S GOING ON, MACK?

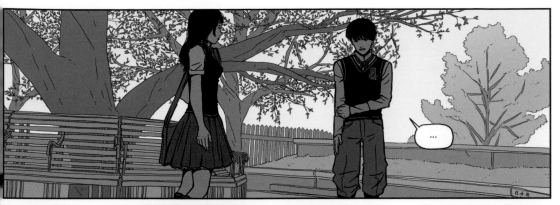

...

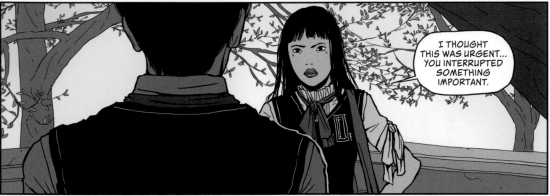

I THOUGHT THIS WAS URGENT... YOU INTERRUPTED SOMETHING IMPORTANT.

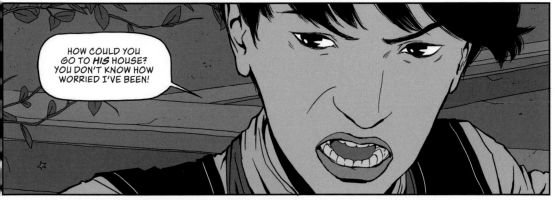

HOW COULD YOU GO TO **HIS** HOUSE? YOU DON'T KNOW HOW WORRIED I'VE BEEN!

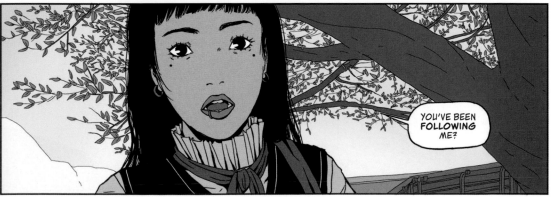

YOU'VE BEEN FOLLOWING ME?

I WANTED TO FIND OUT WHAT YOU WERE UP TO...
WHO DO YOU THINK YOU ARE, MACK?
I *KNOW* WHAT YOU TWO WERE DOING.
I DON'T KNOW WHAT YOU'RE TALKING ABOUT.

HE'S USING YOU!
I'VE HEARD ENOUGH...
JUST LIKE HE DID WITH MY SISTER! DON'T YOU SEE? SHE GOT CLOSE TO HIM AND--
THAT'S ENOUGH, MACK! STAY THE HELL OUT OF MY LIFE!
IF YOU'RE LIVING IN A DREAM, THERE'S ONLY ONE POSSIBLE ENDING...

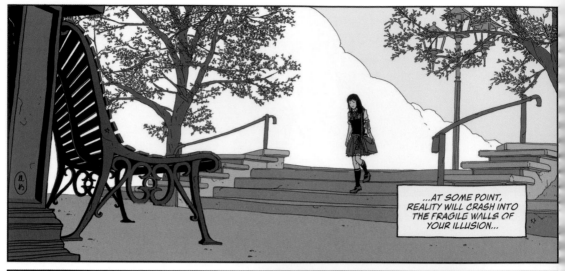

...AT SOME POINT, REALITY WILL CRASH INTO THE FRAGILE WALLS OF YOUR ILLUSION...

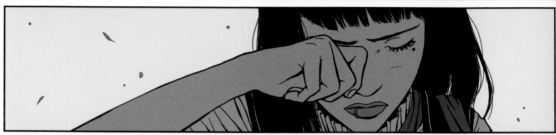

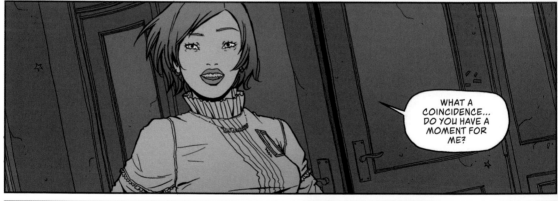

WHAT A COINCIDENCE... DO YOU HAVE A MOMENT FOR ME?

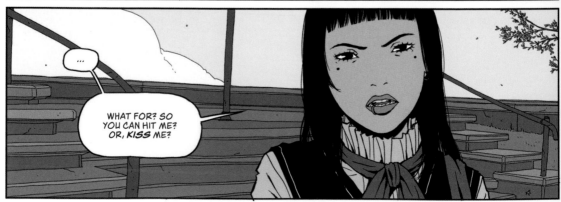

...

WHAT FOR? SO YOU CAN HIT ME? OR, *KISS* ME?

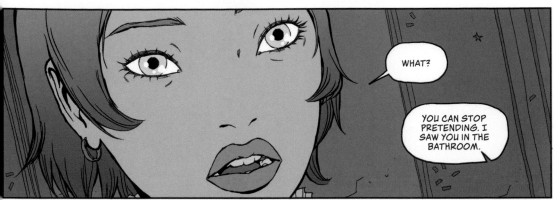

WHAT?

YOU CAN STOP PRETENDING. I SAW YOU IN THE BATHROOM.

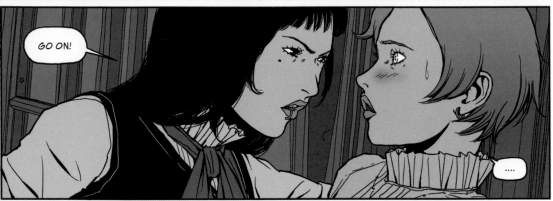

GO ON!

....

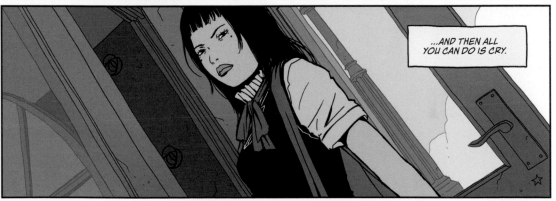

...AND THEN ALL YOU CAN DO IS CRY.

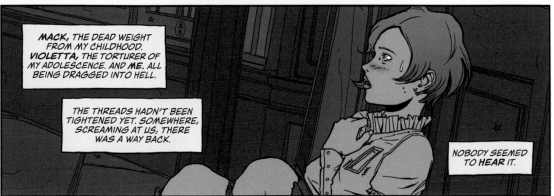

MACK, THE DEAD WEIGHT FROM MY CHILDHOOD. *VIOLETTA*, THE TORTURER OF MY ADOLESCENCE. AND *ME*, ALL BEING DRAGGED INTO HELL.

THE THREADS HADN'T BEEN TIGHTENED YET. SOMEWHERE, SCREAMING AT US, THERE WAS A WAY BACK.

NOBODY SEEMED TO *HEAR* IT.

DON!
I'VE BEEN CALLING YOU...

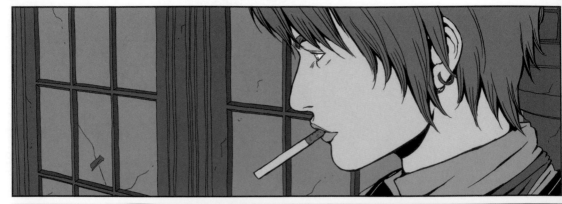

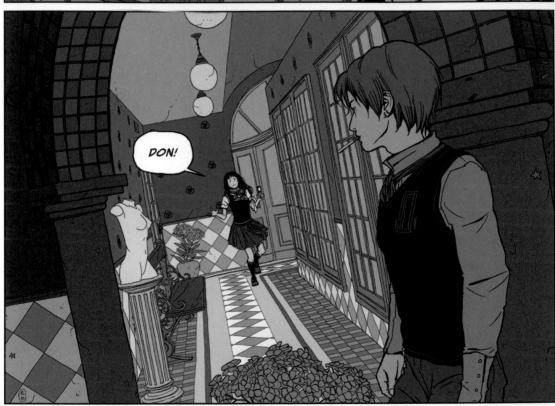

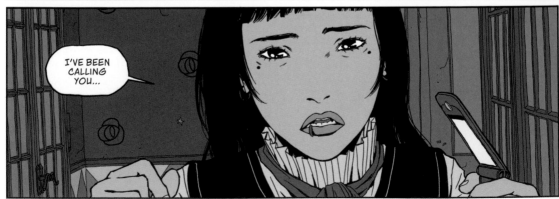

WHAT IS IT?
IT'S MACK. HE FOLLOWED US YESTERDAY. I DON'T KNOW EXACTLY WHAT HE SAW BUT...
...HE SAID, "I KNOW WHAT YOU TWO WERE DOING."
...
DONATIEN, WAIT! DON'T DO ANYTHING TO HIM, ***PLEASE!*** HE'S HAVING A ROUGH TIME--
WE HAVE TO GET ***RID*** OF HIM! HE'S BECOME UNHINGED AFTER THE LOSS OF HIS SISTER, NO SURPRISE THERE. IT'LL BE FAST AND CLEAN.

NO!
WHAT ARE YOU PLAYING AT, EVA?
DON'T YOU REALIZE WHAT THIS MEANS?
WHOSE SIDE ARE YOU ON, HIS OR MINE?
HOW...HOW CAN YOU ASK ME THAT?

DONATIEN!
DONATIEN!

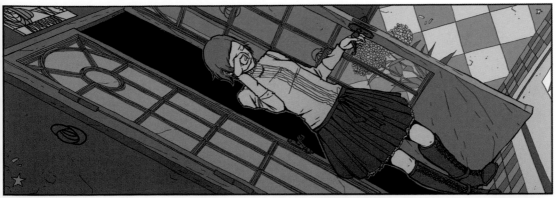

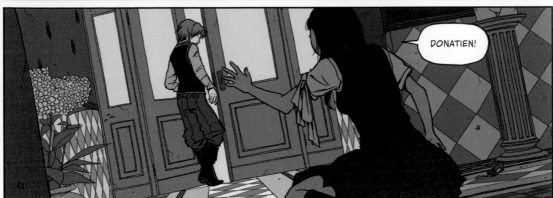

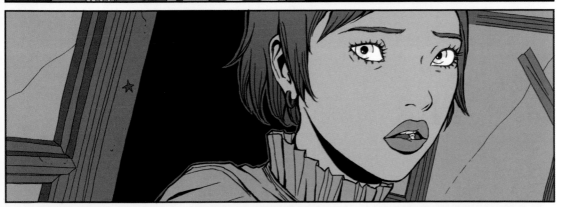

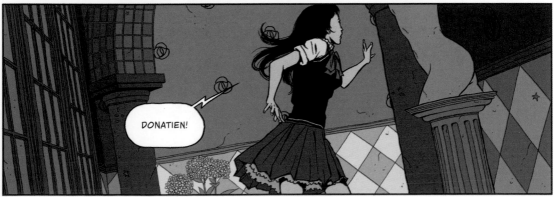

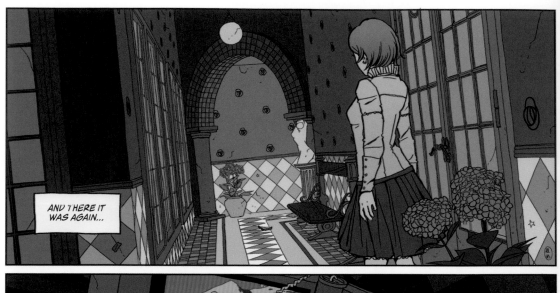

AND THERE IT WAS AGAIN...

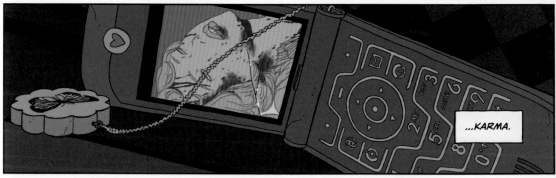

...KARMA.

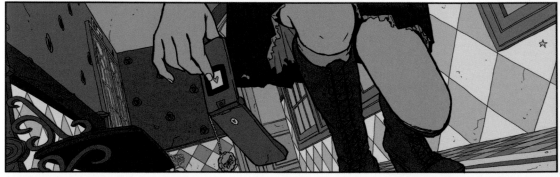

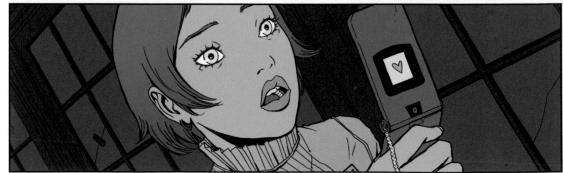

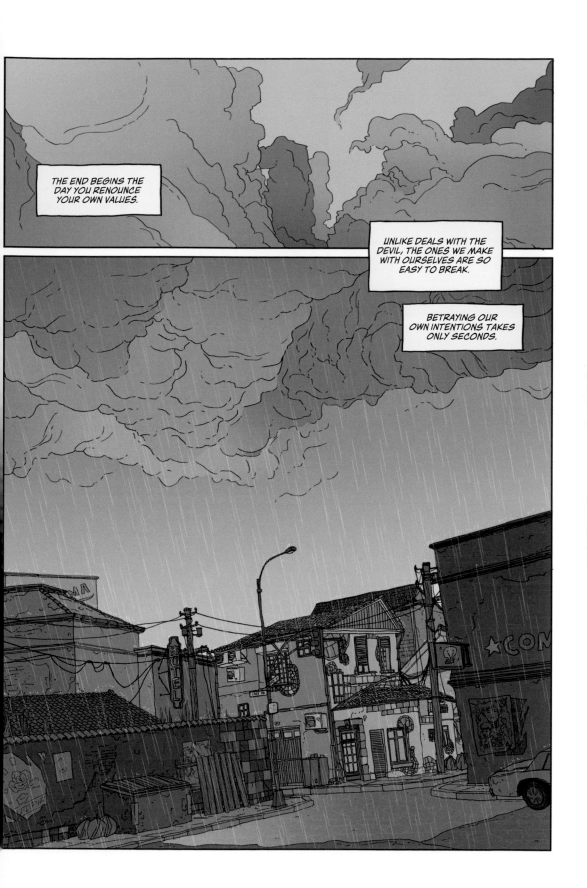

THE END BEGINS THE DAY YOU RENOUNCE YOUR OWN VALUES.

UNLIKE DEALS WITH THE DEVIL, THE ONES WE MAKE WITH OURSELVES ARE SO EASY TO BREAK.

BETRAYING OUR OWN INTENTIONS TAKES ONLY SECONDS.

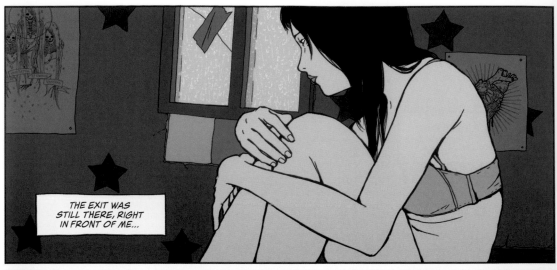

THE EXIT WAS STILL THERE, RIGHT IN FRONT OF ME...

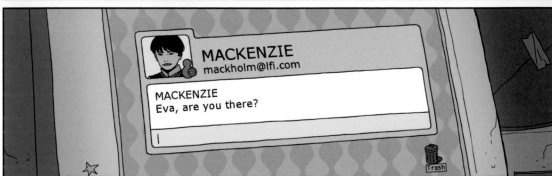

MACKENZIE
mackholm@lfi.com

MACKENZIE
Eva, are you there?

Trash

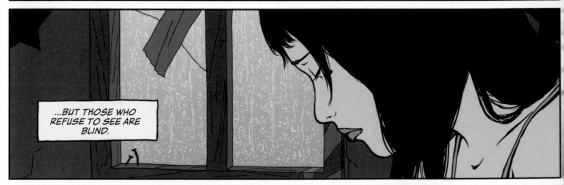

...BUT THOSE WHO REFUSE TO SEE ARE BLIND.

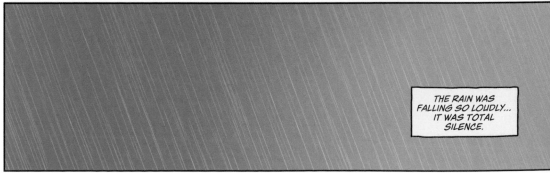

THE RAIN WAS FALLING SO LOUDLY... IT WAS TOTAL SILENCE.

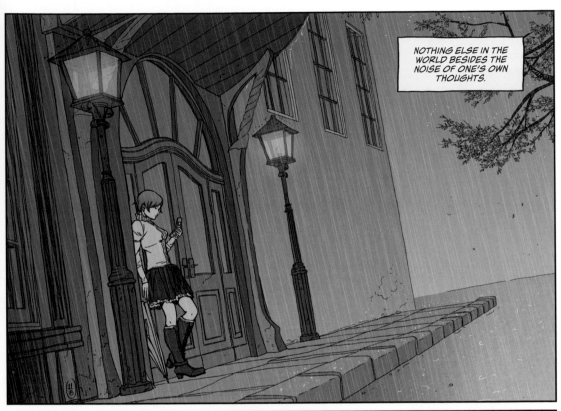

NOTHING ELSE IN THE WORLD BESIDES THE NOISE OF ONE'S OWN THOUGHTS.

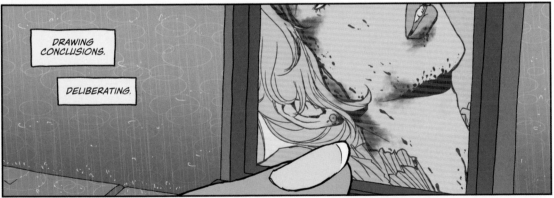

DRAWING CONCLUSIONS.

DELIBERATING.

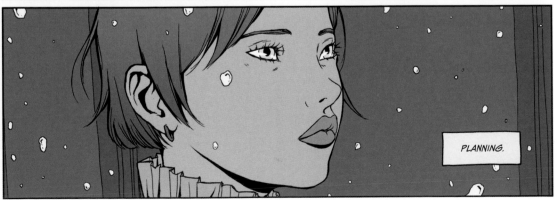

PLANNING.

TORMENTING THE CONSCIENCE.
POISON, STRETCHING OUT ITS BLACK TENTACLES ONCE MORE.

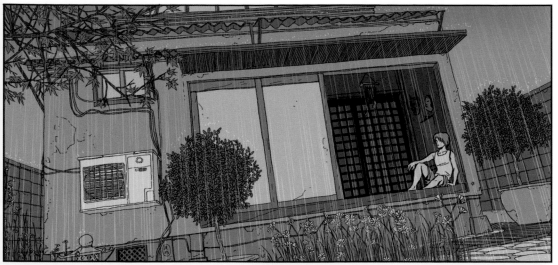

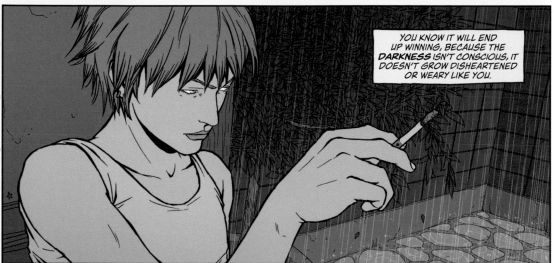

YOU KNOW IT WILL END UP WINNING, BECAUSE THE **DARKNESS** ISN'T CONSCIOUS, IT DOESN'T GROW DISHEARTENED OR WEARY LIKE YOU.

Pii
Pii

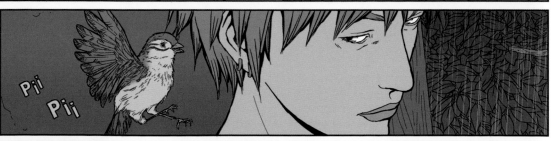

IF YOU DECIMATE ITS NUMBERS, IT DOESN'T **SUFFER** THE WAY YOU DO, BECAUSE IT'S NOT A SINGULAR BEING, BUT ALL BEINGS TO COME.

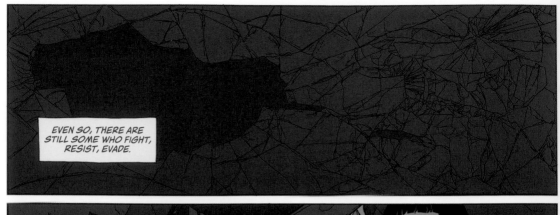

EVEN SO, THERE ARE STILL SOME WHO FIGHT, RESIST, EVADE.

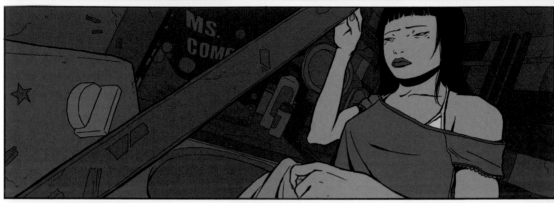

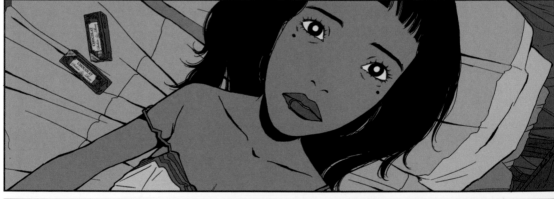

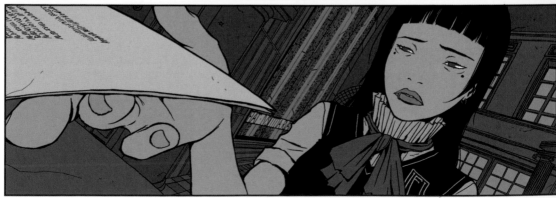

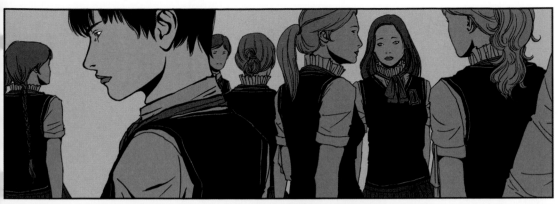

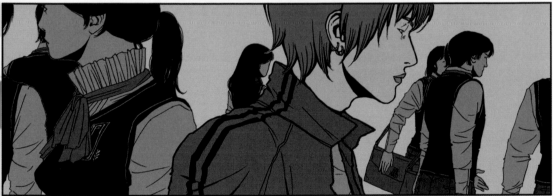

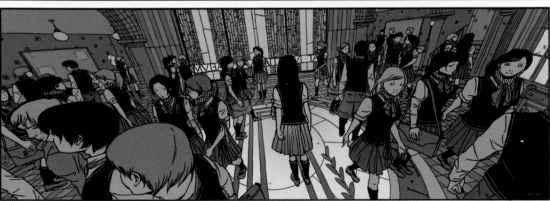

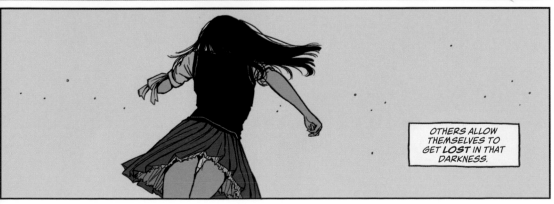

OTHERS ALLOW
THEMSELVES TO
GET **LOST** IN THAT
DARKNESS.

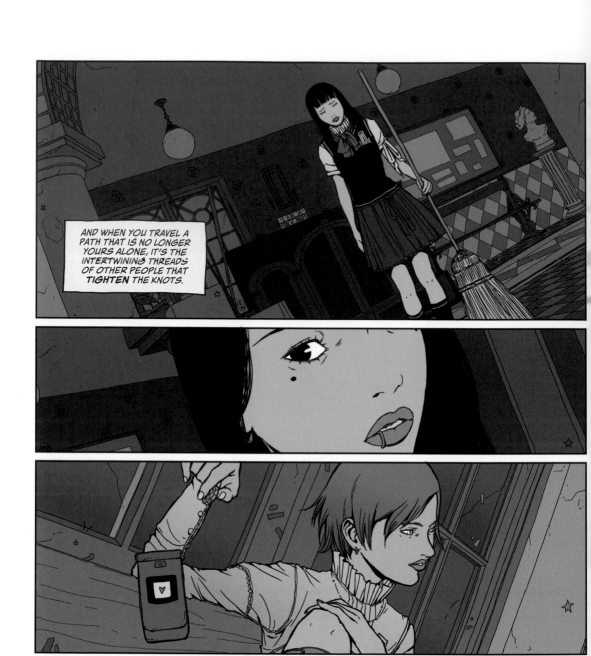

AND WHEN YOU TRAVEL A PATH THAT IS NO LONGER YOURS ALONE, IT'S THE INTERTWINING THREADS OF OTHER PEOPLE THAT **TIGHTEN** THE KNOTS.

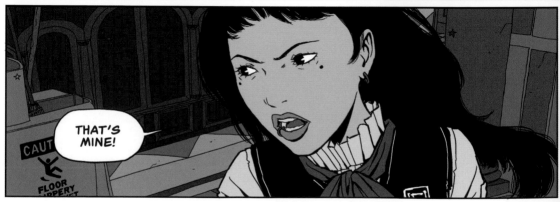

THAT'S MINE!

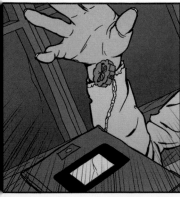
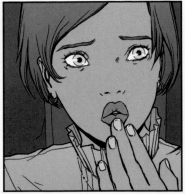
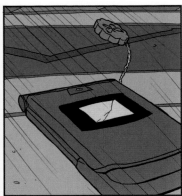
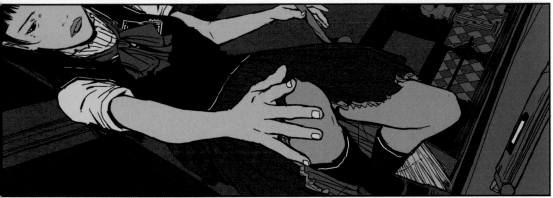
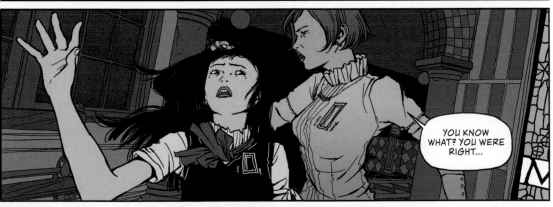

YOU KNOW WHAT? YOU WERE RIGHT...

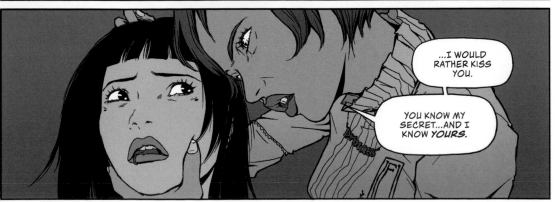

...I WOULD RATHER KISS YOU.

YOU KNOW MY SECRET...AND I KNOW *YOURS*.

IF YOU DON'T WANT THAT PHOTO TO END UP IN THE HEADMISTRESS'S HANDS, YOU'LL DO EVERYTHING I SAY...
AH, KARMA, MY OLD FRIEND...
THINK ABOUT IT. IT'LL BE FUN.
...CRUEL AND UNFORGIVING.

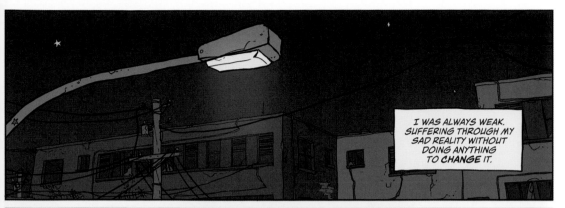

I WAS ALWAYS WEAK, SUFFERING THROUGH MY SAD REALITY WITHOUT DOING ANYTHING TO **CHANGE** IT.

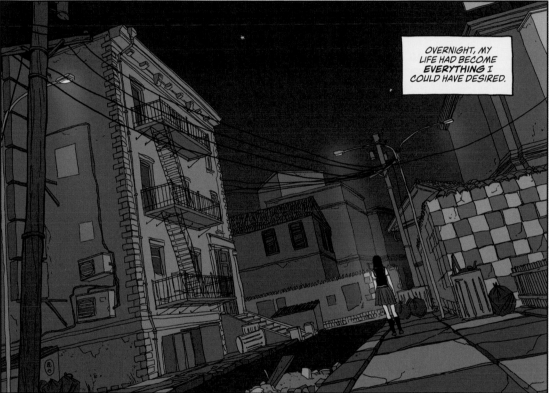

OVERNIGHT, MY LIFE HAD BECOME **EVERYTHING** I COULD HAVE DESIRED.

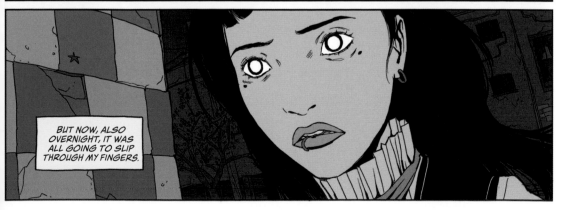

BUT NOW, ALSO OVERNIGHT, IT WAS ALL GOING TO SLIP THROUGH MY FINGERS.

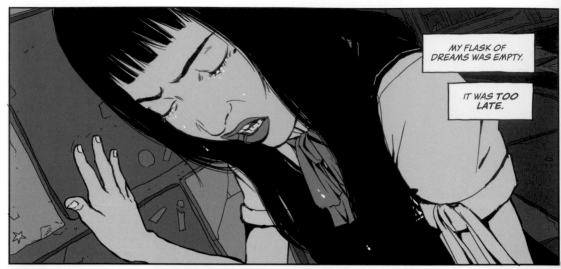

MY FLASK OF DREAMS WAS EMPTY.

IT WAS *TOO* LATE.

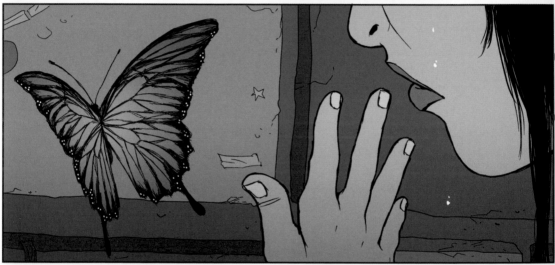

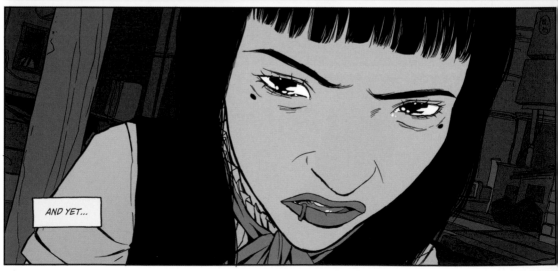

AND YET...

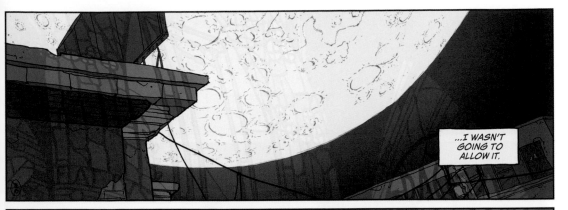

...I WASN'T GOING TO ALLOW IT.

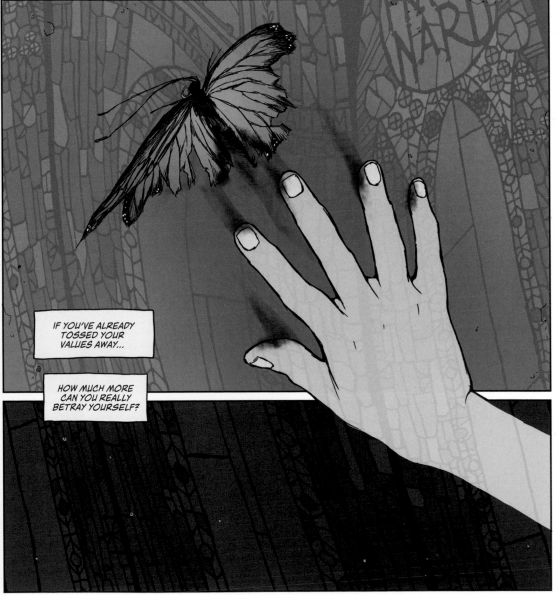

IF YOU'VE ALREADY TOSSED YOUR VALUES AWAY...

HOW MUCH MORE CAN YOU REALLY BETRAY YOURSELF?

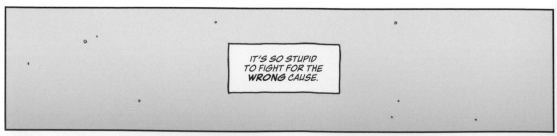

IT'S SO STUPID
TO FIGHT FOR THE
WRONG CAUSE.

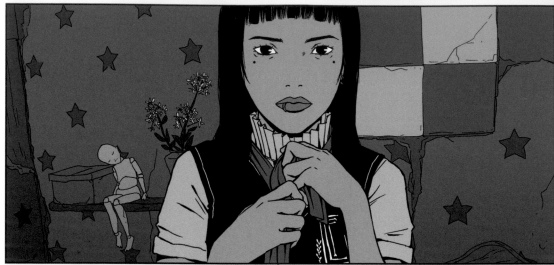

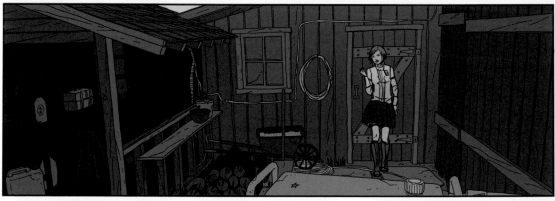

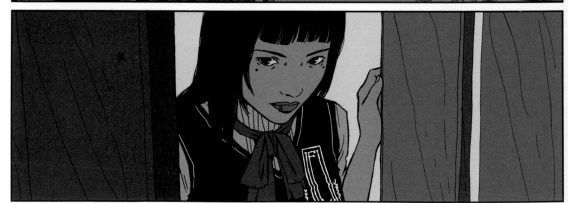

WELL?
I'LL DO WHAT YOU WANT.

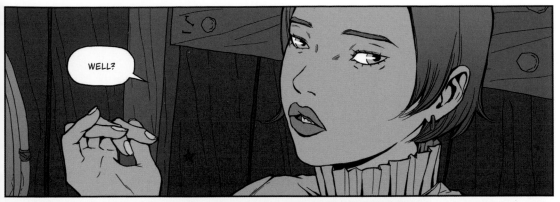

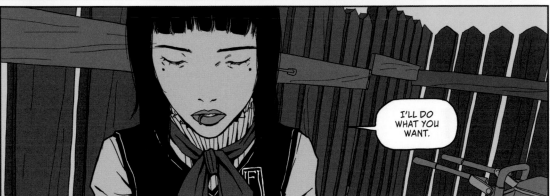

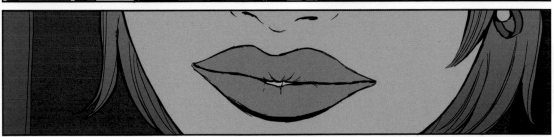

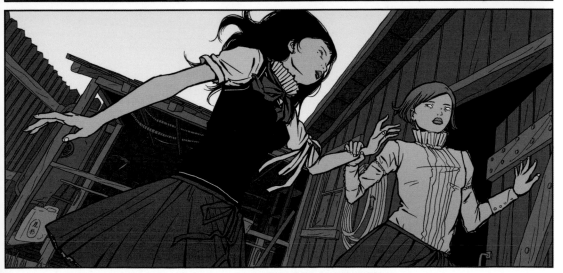

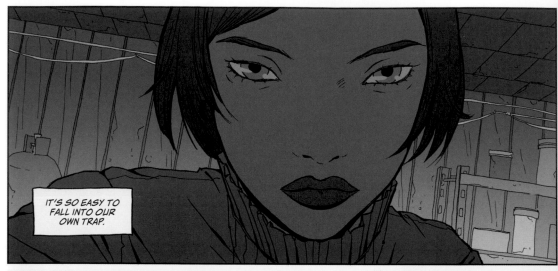

IT'S SO EASY TO FALL INTO OUR OWN TRAP.

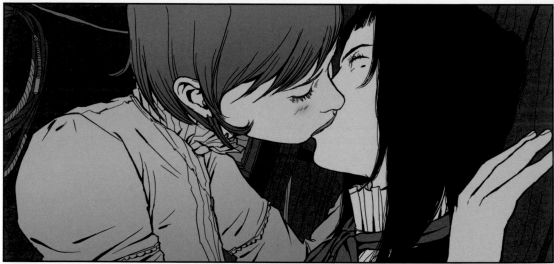

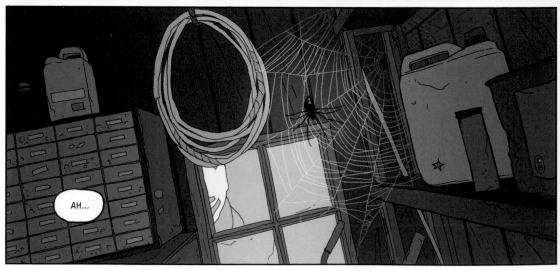

AH...

TEMPTING FATE.
LOSING CONTROL.
IDENTIFYING THE WRONG ENEMY.
WE NEED TO TALK.

YOU WERE RIGHT.

I'M ALWAYS RIGHT...
WE'VE GOT TWO PROBLEMS AND WE NEED TO SOLVE THEM.

DOING THE RIGHT THING IS TOO HARD.
R. N. S19
M. Y. S20
cleaning · クリーニング
reinigen · limpieza
M. Y. S20
V. V. S21
WHAT? THEY CHANGED THE CLEANING ASSIGNMENTS! I'LL HAVE TO STAY...
SEE YOU LATER.

WITH THAT OPTION OUT...
LENO
FIAT·IVSTITIA·RVAT·CAELVM
FRAGONARD
...ONLY THE **EASY** WAY REMAINS.
MACK, I DON'T WANT US TO GO ON LIKE THIS. I'VE GOT CLEANING DUTY. CAN YOU COME LATER? PLEASE, LET'S FIX THIS.

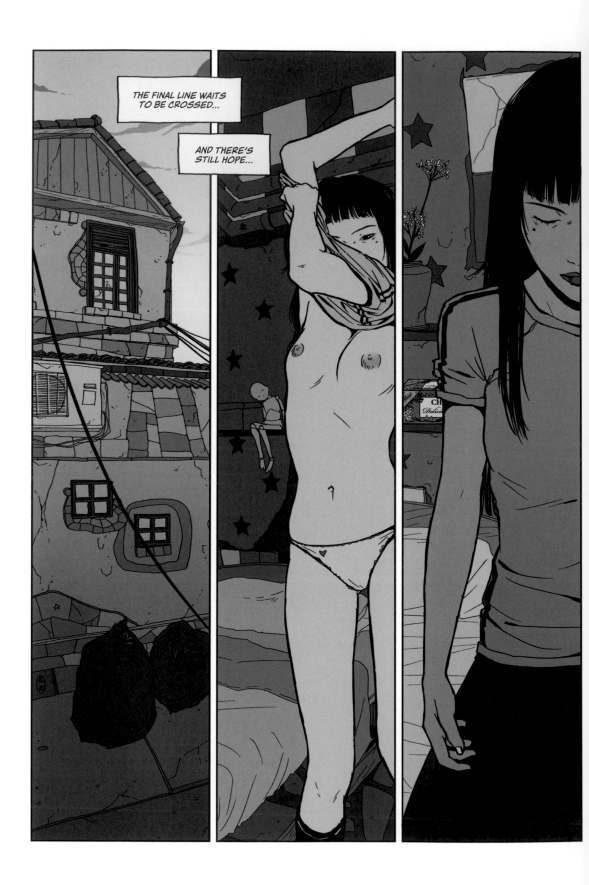

THE FINAL LINE WAITS
TO BE CROSSED...

AND THERE'S
STILL HOPE...

122

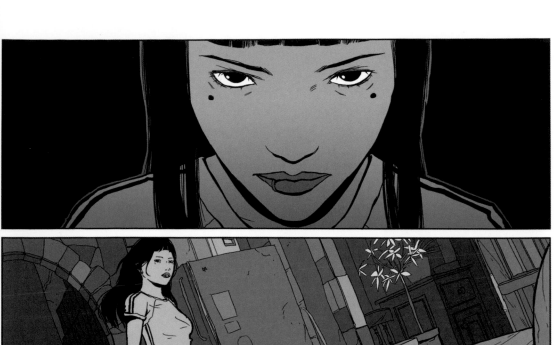

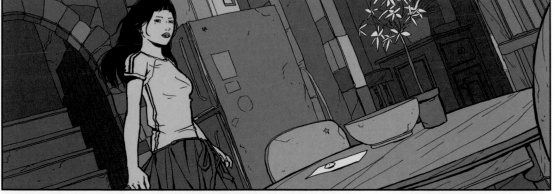

BUT THE THING
YOU'VE BEEN WAITING
SO LONG FOR...

Eva,

I'll be home
early today!

We can order in
and eat together
for once! :)

Love you,
Mom

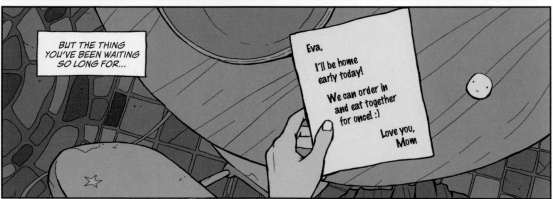

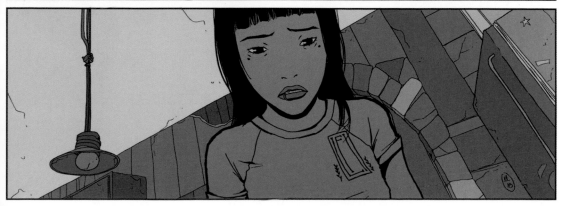

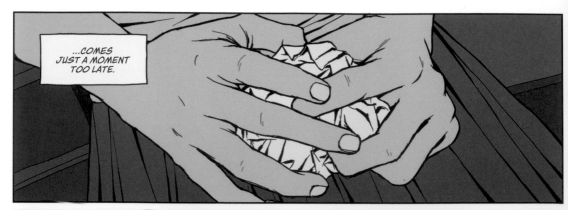

...COMES JUST A MOMENT TOO LATE.

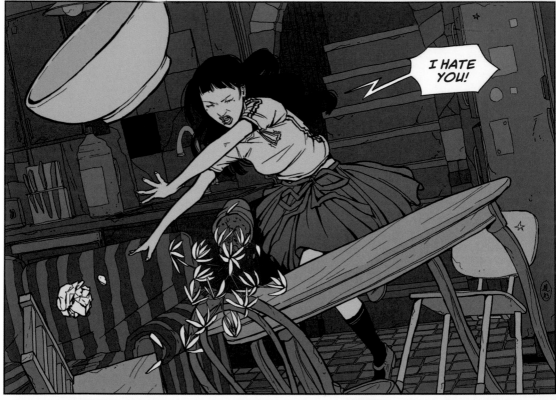

I HATE YOU!

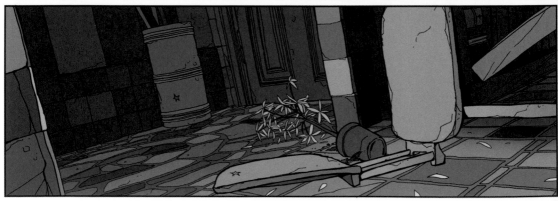

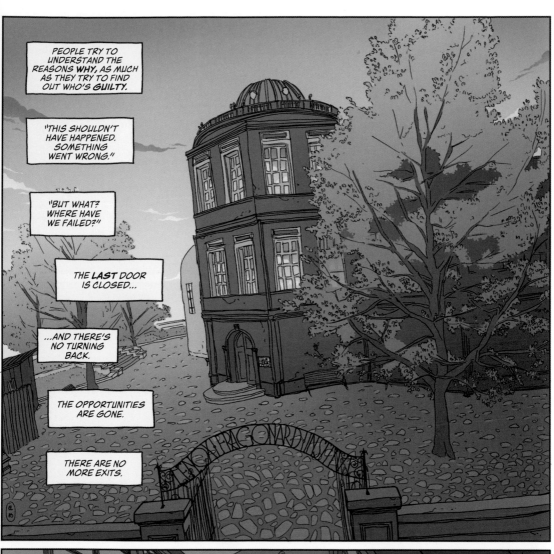

PEOPLE TRY TO
UNDERSTAND THE
REASONS **WHY**, AS MUCH
AS THEY TRY TO FIND
OUT WHO'S **GUILTY**.

"THIS SHOULDN'T
HAVE HAPPENED.
SOMETHING
WENT WRONG."

"BUT WHAT?
WHERE HAVE
WE FAILED?"

THE **LAST** DOOR
IS CLOSED...

...AND THERE'S
NO TURNING
BACK.

THE OPPORTUNITIES
ARE GONE.

THERE ARE NO
MORE EXITS.

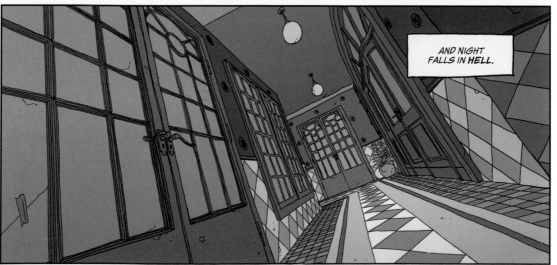

AND NIGHT
FALLS IN **HELL**.

AH!

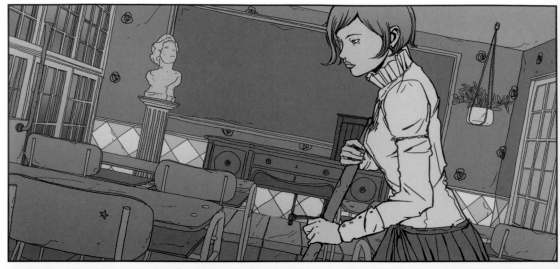

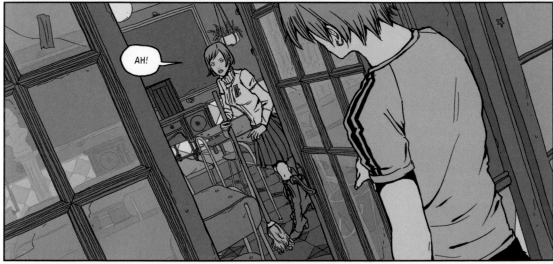

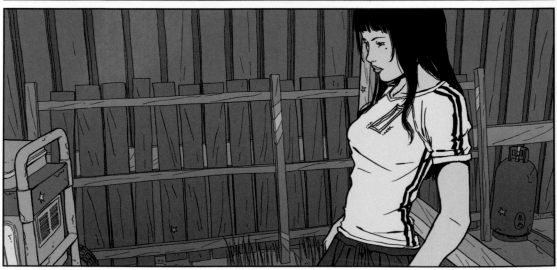

MACK!
YOU SCARED ME...
Princess

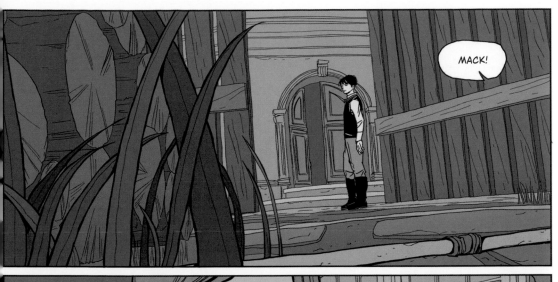

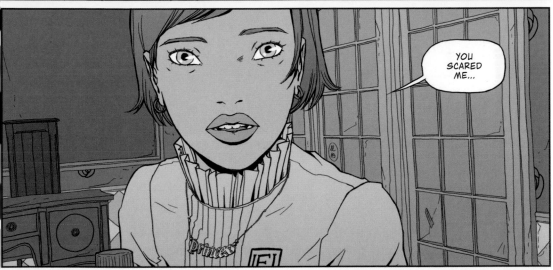

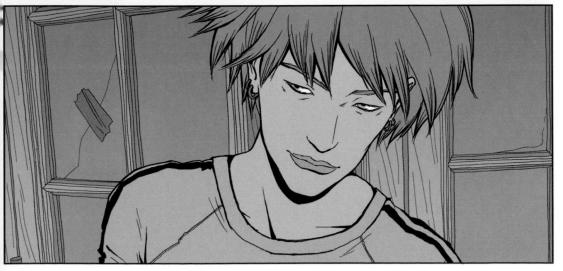

THANKS FOR COMING.
NO PROBLEM.
MACK...I'M SORRY. I DON'T WANT TO KEEP FIGHTING.
WE SHOULD GET ALONG... FOR OLD TIMES' SAKE.

SO, YOU'VE TAKEN UP BLACKMAIL.
WHAT? THAT'S RIDICULOUS...
WHY WOULD I DO THAT?
DON'T *LIE*, YOU'RE NOT THAT GOOD AT IT.

I KNOW THINGS ARE ROUGH FOR YOU RIGHT NOW...
BUT YOU NEED TO RELAX...GET THOSE CRAZY IDEAS OUT OF YOUR HEAD...
THIS IS WHY YOU WANTED ME TO COME? MY SISTER WOULDN'T LISTEN TO ME EITHER...
AMBER AND I ARE COMPLETELY DIFFERENT, MACK.
HE'S DOING THE SAME THING TO YOU THAT HE DID TO HER!

YOU KNOW, THERE'S SOMETHING YOU HAVEN'T THOUGHT OF...WHEN EVA TOOK THAT PHOTO...
ISN'T IT POSSIBLE, EVEN *LIKELY,* THAT SHE SAW THE KILLER?
princess

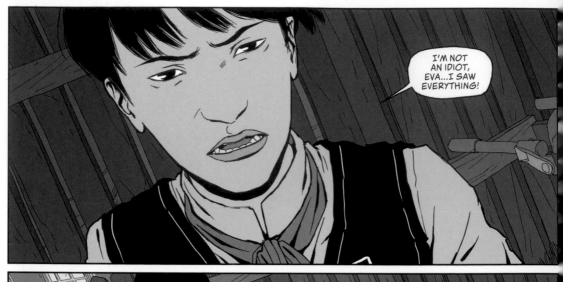

I'M NOT AN IDIOT, EVA...I SAW EVERYTHING!

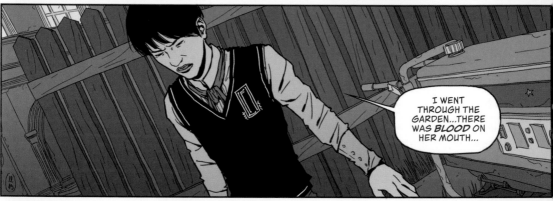

I WENT THROUGH THE GARDEN...THERE WAS *BLOOD* ON HER MOUTH...

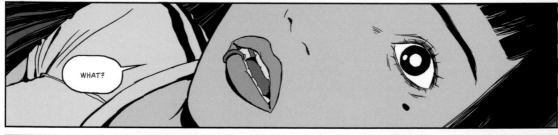

WHAT?

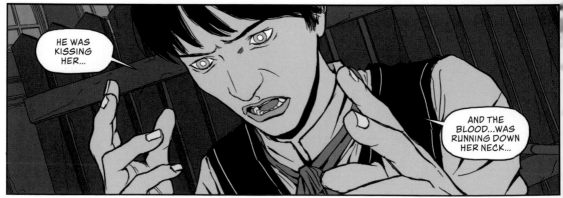

HE WAS KISSING HER...

AND THE BLOOD...WAS RUNNING DOWN HER NECK...

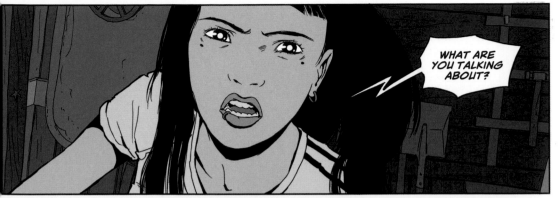

WHAT ARE YOU TALKING ABOUT?

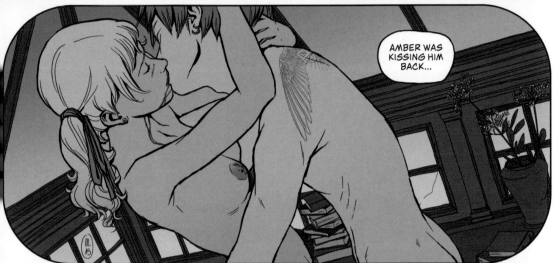

AMBER WAS KISSING HIM BACK...

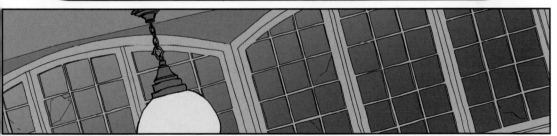

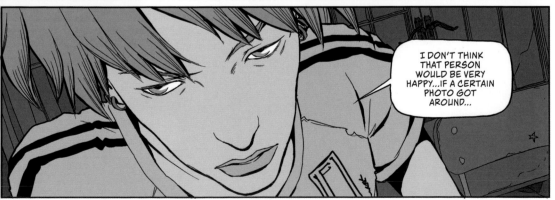

I DON'T THINK THAT PERSON WOULD BE VERY HAPPY...IF A CERTAIN PHOTO GOT AROUND...

NO! SHE...IT WAS ONLY...HER HEARTBEAT...WAS POUNDING SO LOUD... IT WAS JUST--
YOU THINK YOU'RE *SPECIAL,* DON'T YOU?
YOU DON'T UNDERSTAND! I SAW IT WITH MY OWN EYES! I SAW HIM! HE *LOVES* ME!
HE LOVES YOU?

YOU'RE SCARING ME...
AM I?
DON'T YOU REALIZE, EVA? YOU'RE GOING TO BE NEXT!

SHUT UP!

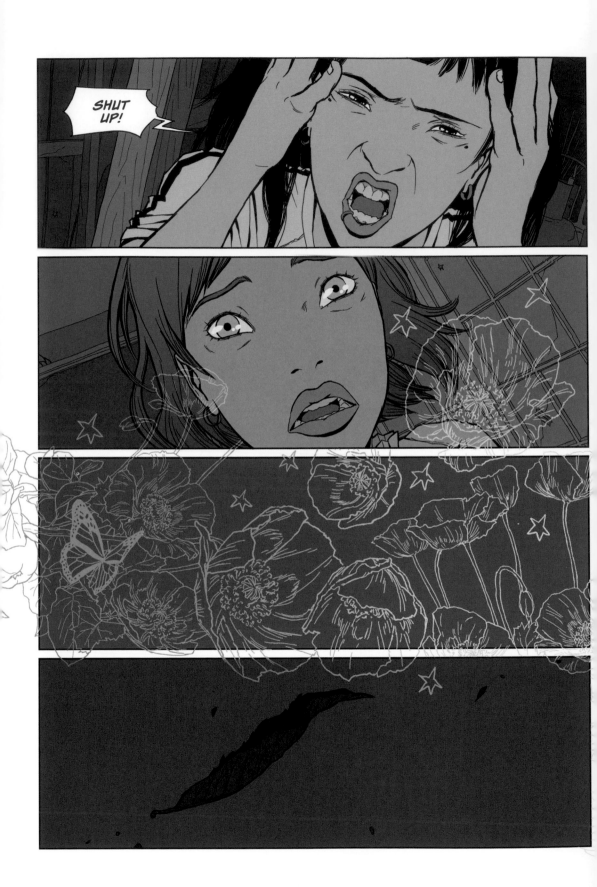

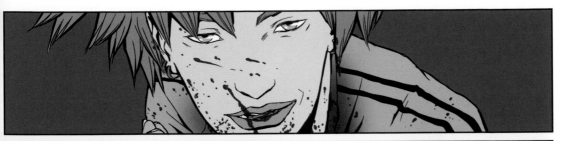

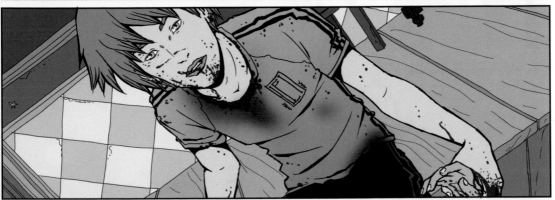

ARE YOU GOING TO KILL ME?

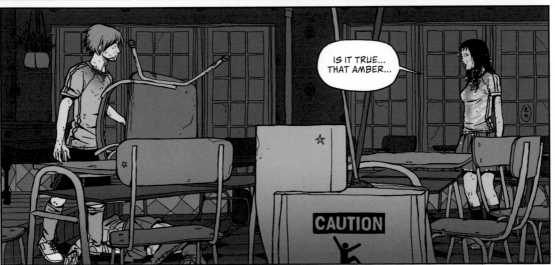

IS IT TRUE... THAT AMBER...

CAUTION

I THOUGHT I WAS SPECIAL...
...
HOW COULD I HURT YOU?

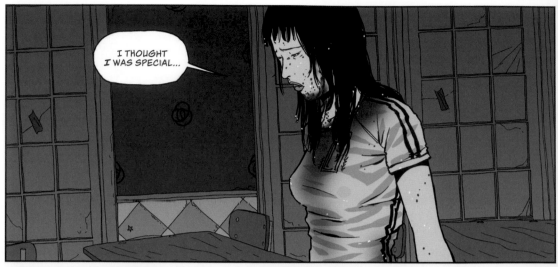

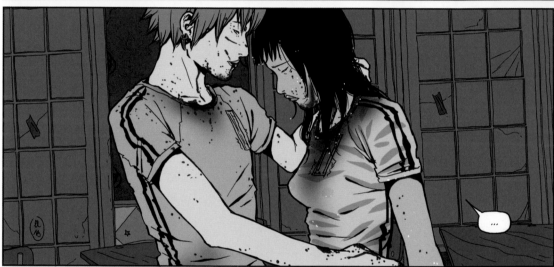

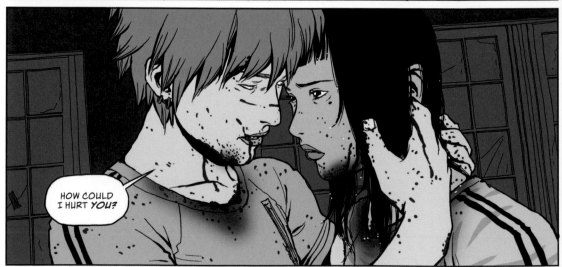

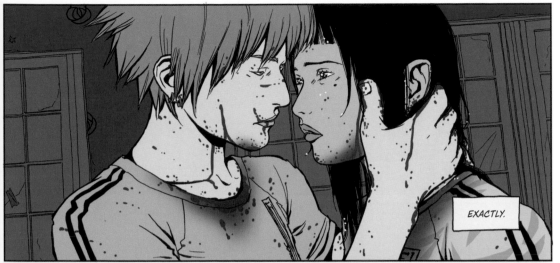

EXACTLY.

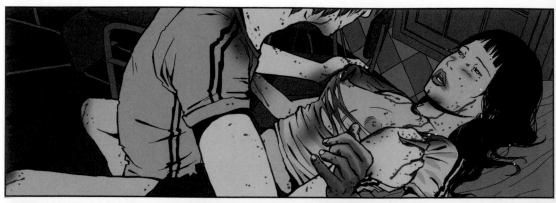

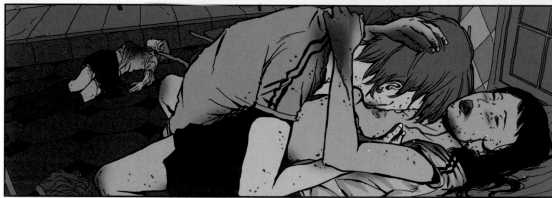

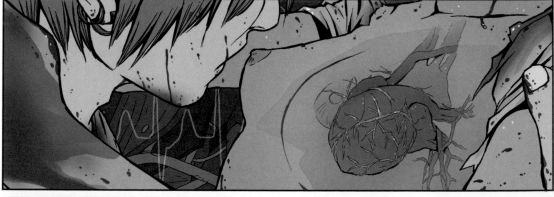

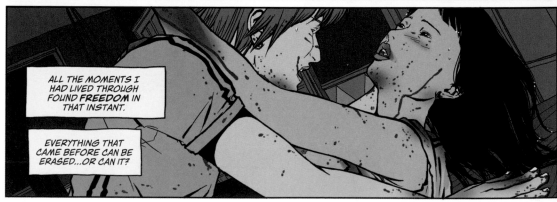

ALL THE MOMENTS I
HAD LIVED THROUGH
FOUND **FREEDOM** IN
THAT INSTANT.

EVERYTHING THAT
CAME BEFORE CAN BE
ERASED...OR CAN IT?

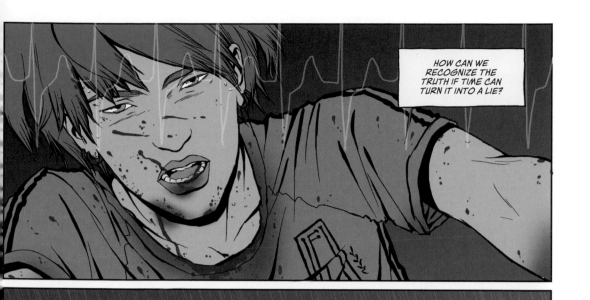

HOW CAN WE RECOGNIZE THE TRUTH IF TIME CAN TURN IT INTO A LIE?

WHO IS GUILTY? WHO IS TO BLAME?

MY MOTHER.

DIDN'T SHE DESPISE HERSELF AS MUCH AS THE SNOBS SHE SERVED DID? SHE FORCED ME INTO SOLITUDE, REJECTION, SADNESS! WHAT DOES IT MATTER WHAT HER REASONS WERE?

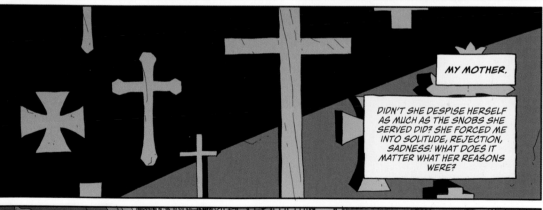

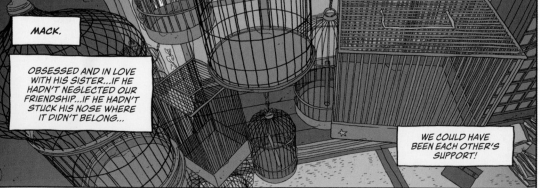

MACK.

OBSESSED AND IN LOVE WITH HIS SISTER...IF HE HADN'T NEGLECTED OUR FRIENDSHIP...IF HE HADN'T STUCK HIS NOSE WHERE IT DIDN'T BELONG...

WE COULD HAVE BEEN EACH OTHER'S SUPPORT!

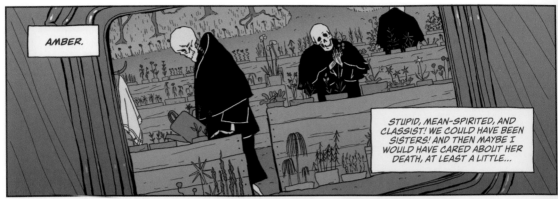

AMBER.

STUPID, MEAN-SPIRITED, AND CLASSIST! WE COULD HAVE BEEN SISTERS! AND THEN MAYBE I WOULD HAVE CARED ABOUT HER DEATH, AT LEAST A LITTLE...

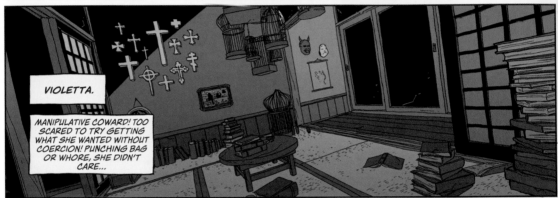

VIOLETTA.

MANIPULATIVE COWARD! TOO SCARED TO TRY GETTING WHAT SHE WANTED WITHOUT COERCION! PUNCHING BAG OR WHORE, SHE DIDN'T CARE...

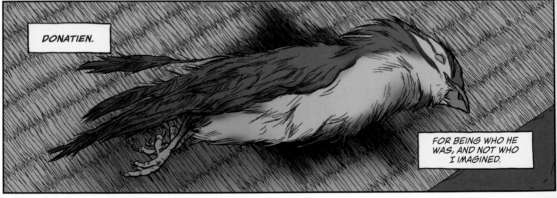

DONATIEN.

FOR BEING WHO HE WAS, AND NOT WHO I IMAGINED.

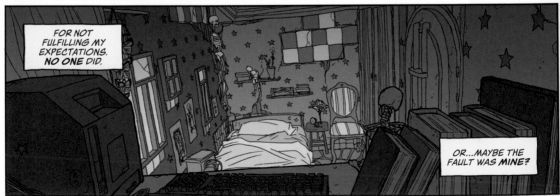

FOR NOT FULFILLING MY EXPECTATIONS. NO ONE DID.

OR...MAYBE THE FAULT WAS MINE?

WHEN THEY SAY, "SOMETIMES IT'S SIMPLY NOBODY'S FAULT..."
MAYBE IN REALITY...
...THEY'RE ONLY TRYING TO AVOID THE FACT...

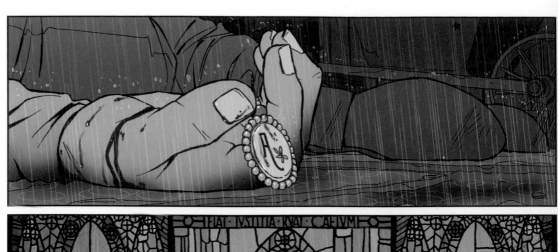

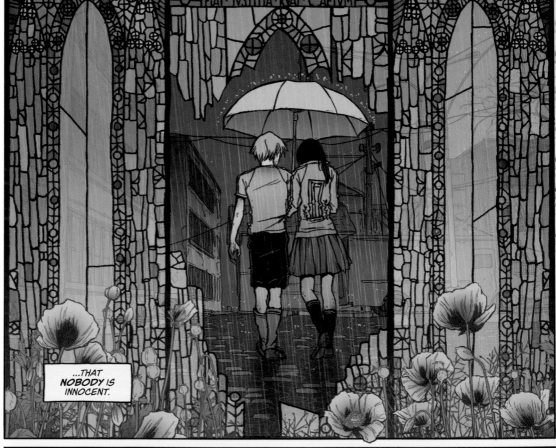

...THAT *NOBODY* IS INNOCENT.

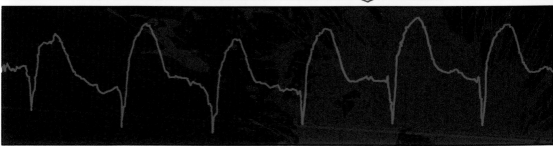

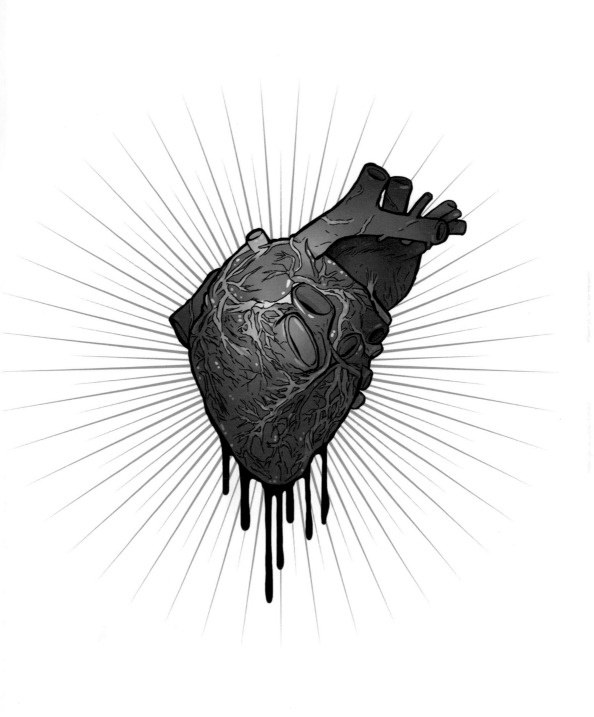

COVER GALLERY

Heartbeat Main Covers by **MARIA LLOVET**

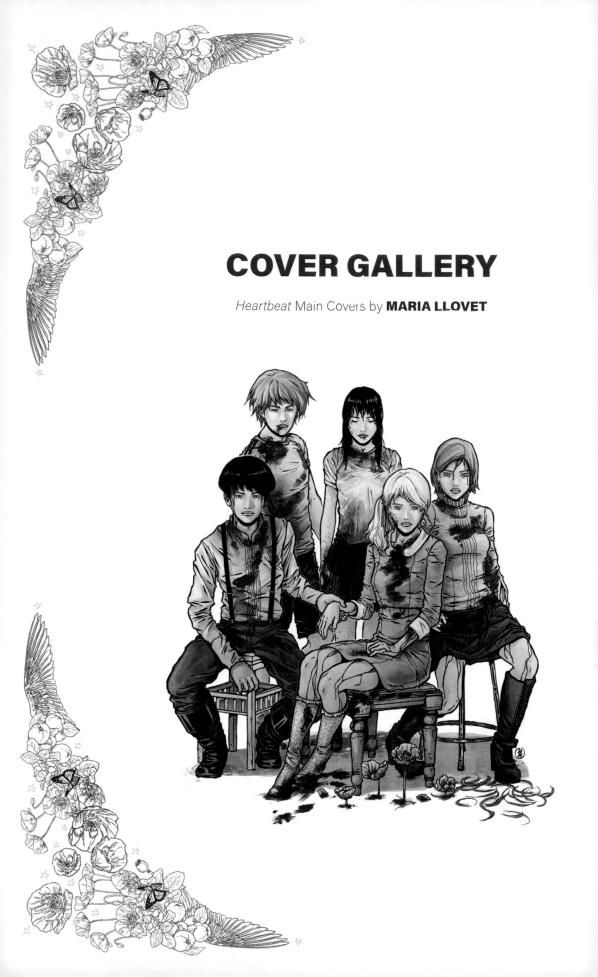

MARIA LLOVET 2019

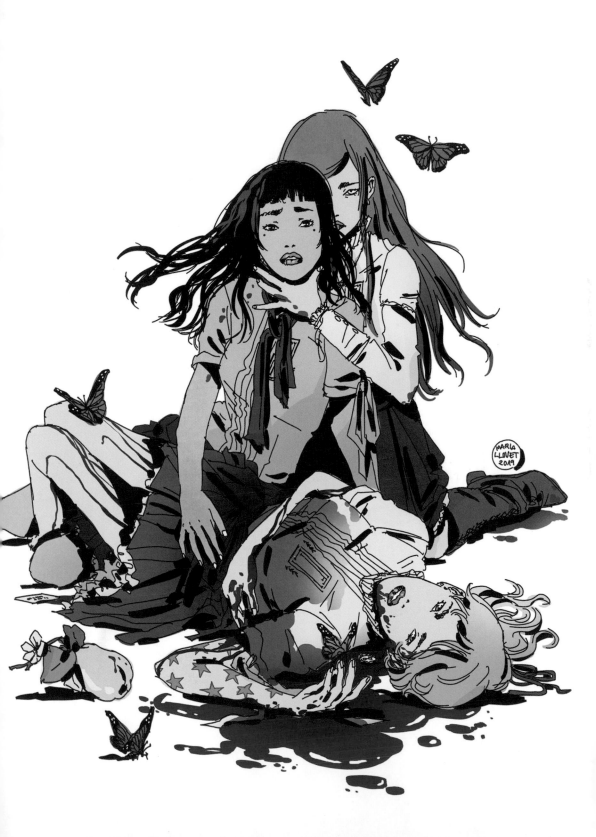

MARIA LLOVET 2019

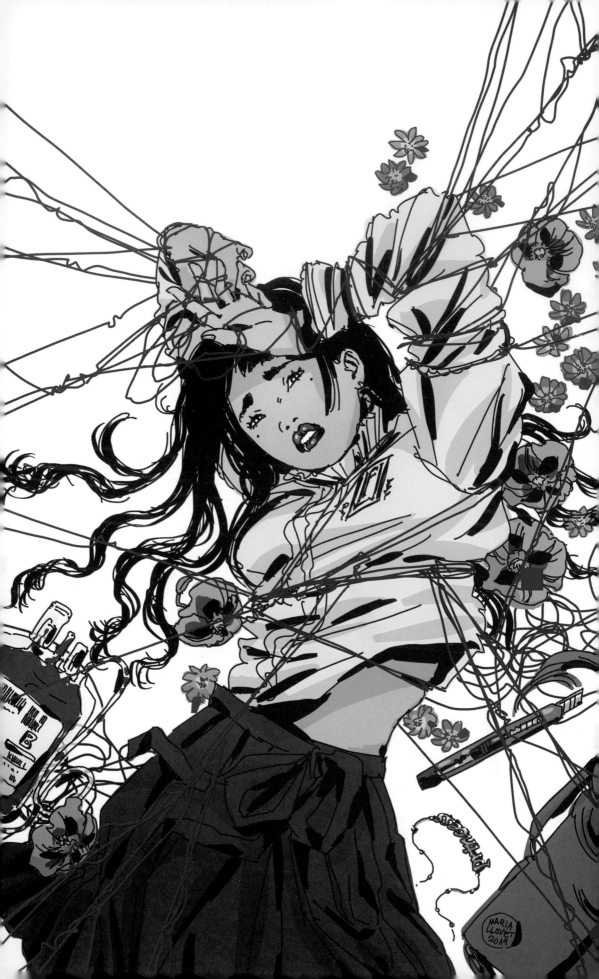

MARIA
LLOVET
2019

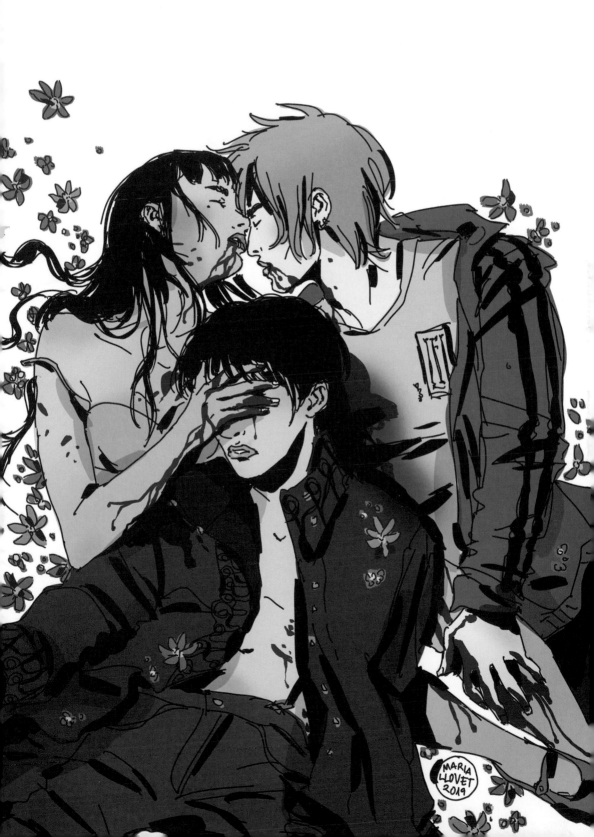

MARIA
LLOVET
2019

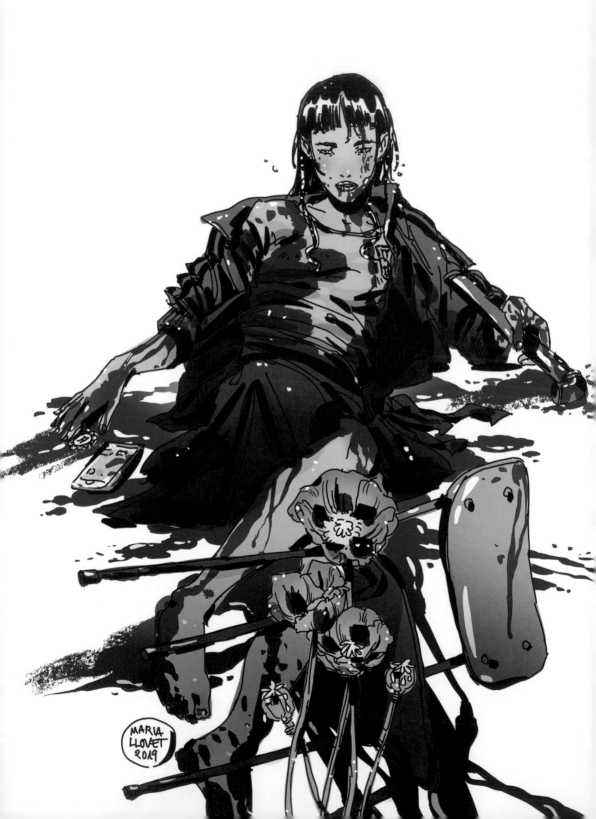

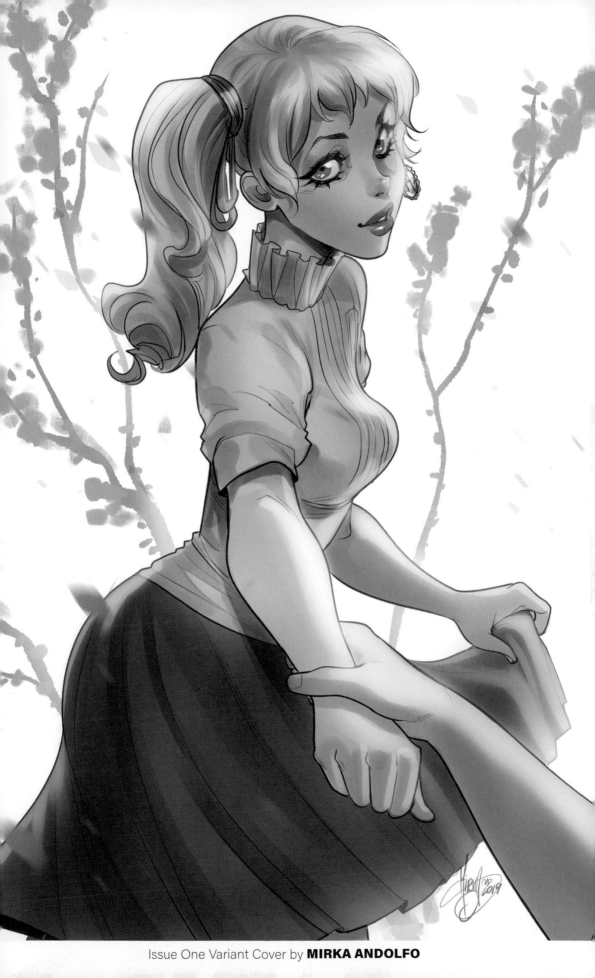

Issue One Variant Cover by **MIRKA ANDOLFO**

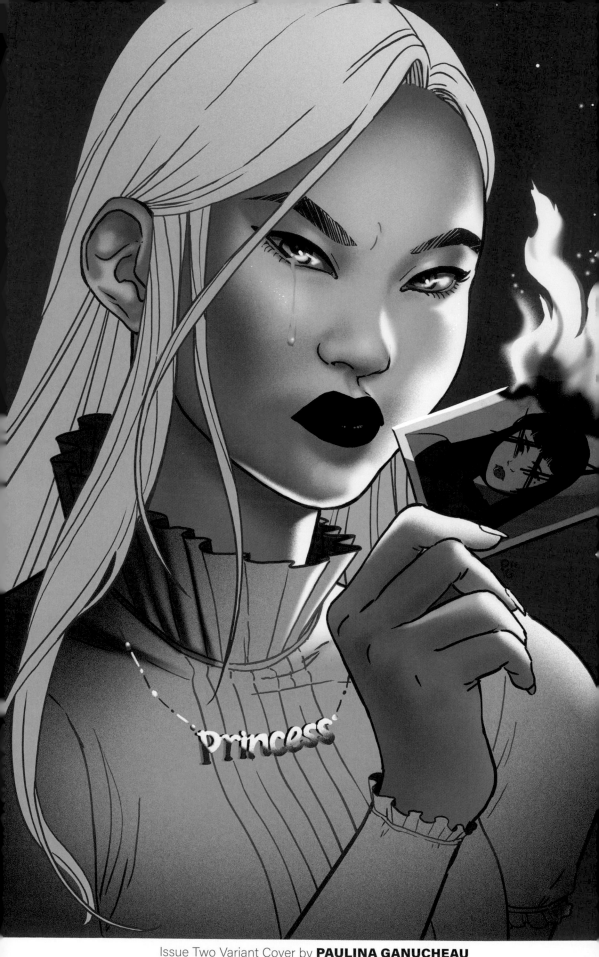

Issue Two Variant Cover by **PAULINA GANUCHEAU**

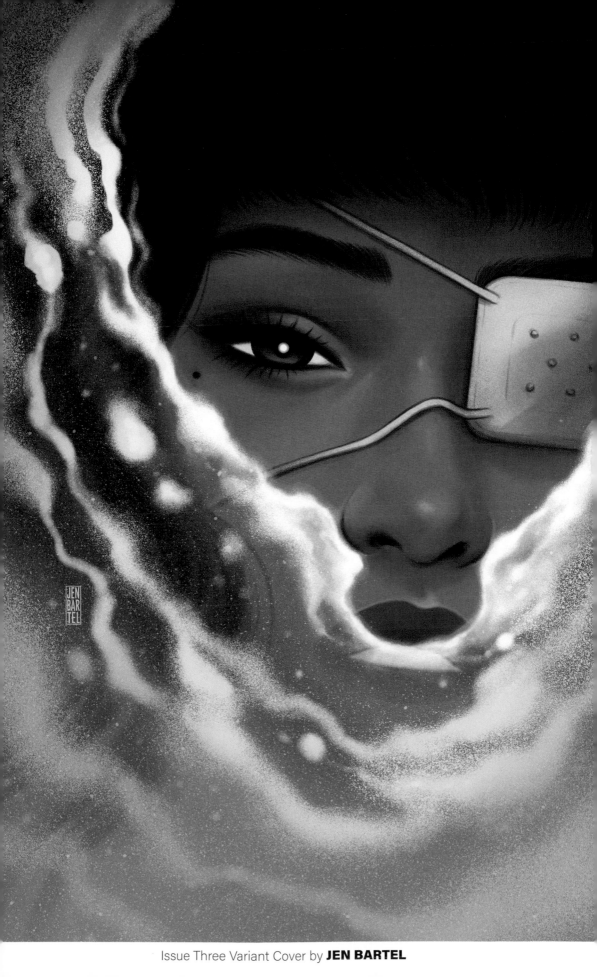

Issue Three Variant Cover by **JEN BARTEL**

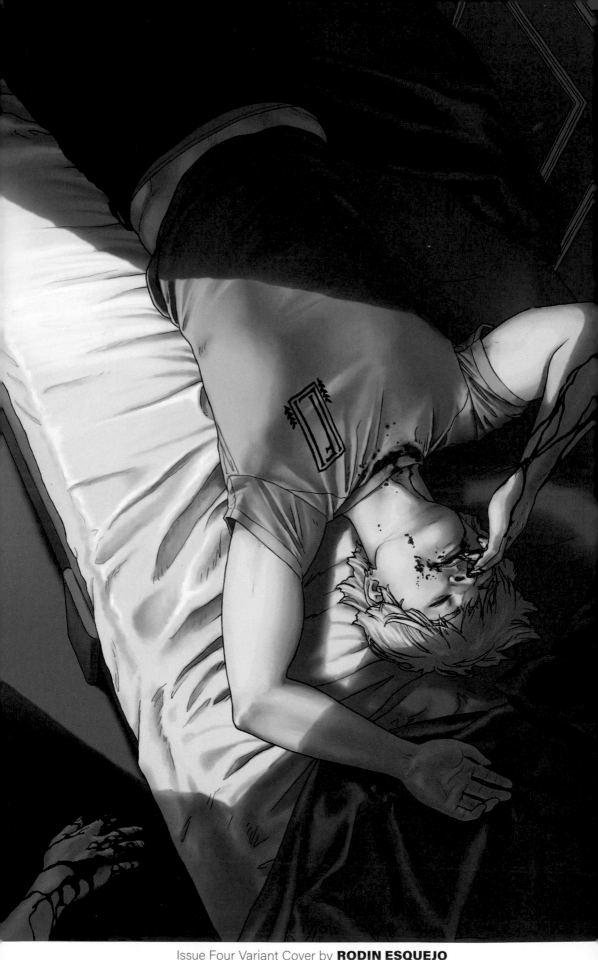

Issue Four Variant Cover by **RODIN ESQUEJO**

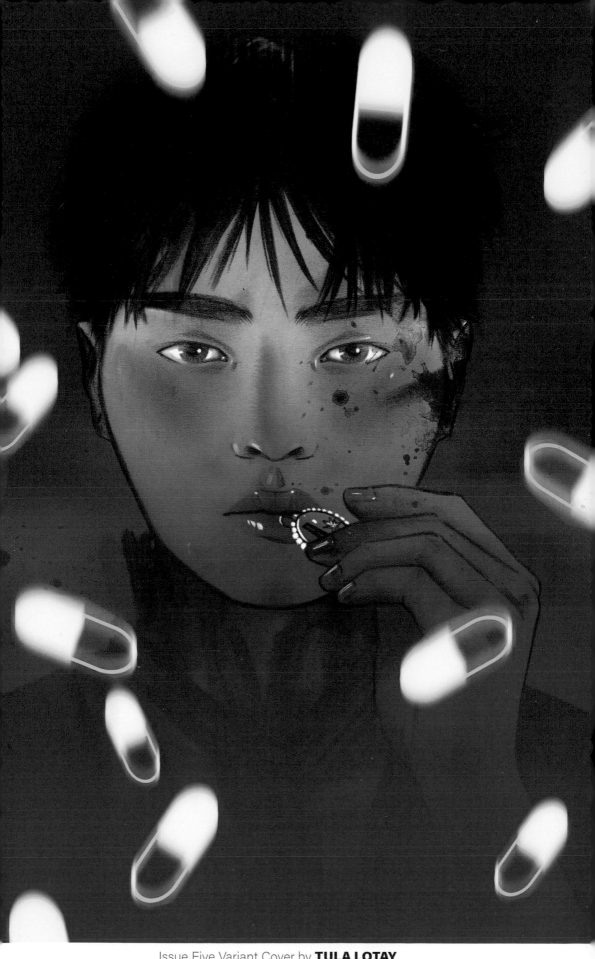

Issue Five Variant Cover by **TULA LOTAY**

MEMENTO · MORI

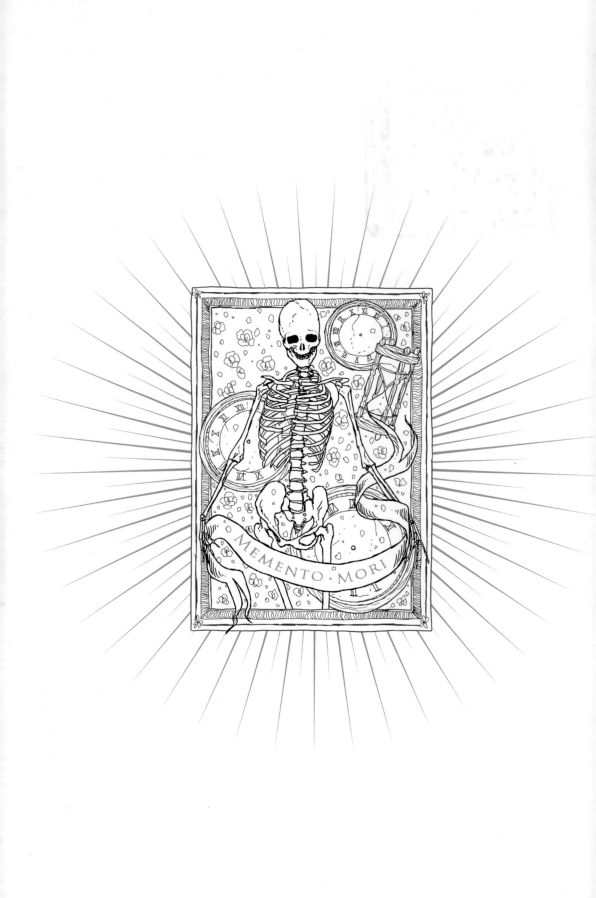